Fields of
Orange
A True Welsh Love Story

Fields of Orange

Orange

A True Welsh Love Story

Johanna Francis

with Jantien Powell & Alan Francis
Edited by Stephen Jones

First impression: 2022

© Copyright Alan Francis & Jantien Powell and Y Lolfa Cyf., 2022

Cover design: Y Lolfa
Cover image: Private Collection

The publishers wish to acknowledge the support
of the Books Council of Wales

ISBN: 978 1 80099 146 0

Published and printed in Wales
on paper from well-maintained forests by
Y Lolfa Cyf., Talybont, Ceredigion SY24 5HE
website www.ylolfa.com
e-mail ylolfa@ylolfa.com
tel 01970 832 304
fax 832 782

Contents

Editor's note

IT WAS DURING my college days that I first met Hanny Francis. Alan, her son, and I both went to Oxford Polytechnic, now Oxford Brookes University, in the years when further education was underfunded, a little hand to mouth and, frankly, scruffy. Like the students.

Al drove us down to Wales one day and, after introductions at his house, Hanny – who, frankly, looked ravishing and always continued to do so – laid on the warmest of Welsh welcomes and the largest of lunches.

It was only later that I discovered all the layers of Hanny's life. Over the years it was known that she was writing. She kept her words a secret until not long before she died, but Alan and Jantien, her daughter, knew that she was noting down her memories, sometimes with periods when the words flowed beautifully and other times when she struggled to find those words.

To be the first to read her words was a great honour. To discover the astonishing story of Hanny and Bob, Holland and Wales, love and struggle, feast and famine, and especially of two families, was an absolute delight.

Most of the text was never saved on computers, so we always dreaded a small fire.

She once wrote:

A few months have passed again without me writing a word. It is February and I thought I would do a lot more writing during the dark winter months, but the trouble is that one has to be in a writing mood; that means sitting down for an hour or so, which I find very hard, especially during the day.

It has been like that ever since I started writing this story of my life. I have always been a 'do-er', busy all day long doing jobs in the house or outside, until at least 7pm. If that happens then I feel I have filled my day with something useful (not always!) and can relax for the evening watching television or having a go on the computer – although the latter causes me a lot of stress!

As we are in the age of technology, I felt some time ago I should definitely have a go at learning how to use a computer, or I might be left behind. I did have a computer before, an old one from Al's office. I muddled along with that one for a while and became quite good at it.

Then, last Christmas [2014], Al and Jant bought me a new laptop! Oh boy, was I excited, not realising the turbulent road ahead of me. It has just been so frustrating. The new laptop is right up to date, but I seem unable to do all the tricks, not even the things that I used to do on my old computer, which is now obsolete. But I will persevere. It's just so frustrating; it makes me bad-tempered. I'll get there eventually... the question is, when?

And the answer, dear Hanny? Now!

Stephen Jones
March 2022

Part I

Hanny's Memoir

Hell's Neighbour

IN 1936, THE year in which I was born, my family moved across Amsterdam to a house in Oranje Nassaulaan, a street named after the Dutch royal family. It is one of the longest streets in Amsterdam, and runs into the beautiful Vondelpark which is now a national monument.

I was named Johanna, just one Christian name, although all my sisters and brothers had more than one name. This was decided because I had two aunts, both called Johanna, so to prevent any argument I was given one name so they would both think I was named after them.

The house was very grand, spacious and beautiful, probably even baronial. Several grand pianos nestled themselves in its hidden depths. It was of a type called *herenhuis* or in English, 'gentleman's house'. It had a wealth of features on six floors and was enormous. It had to be. I was the fifth child born to Herman Fokke Dooyeweerd and Jantiena Dooyeweerd (née Fernhout). I joined Mieke, Marja, Eveliene and Herman; and after me, we were to be augmented by Frederika, Tineke, Joop and Arnold. All at intervals of roughly two years.

Our father was a professor at Vrije University. If we had

known in 1940, after the German invasion of Holland and the Low Countries, the feared Gestapo would set up their headquarters across the road, my family might not have felt quite so blessed.

There was great danger and uncertainty to come in our lives. We also had various nooks and crannies in the house where those sought by the Gestapo could secret themselves, almost under German noses. The Gestapo, our hellish neighbours, were suspicious of us. My father was called in several times to their headquarters. There was also terrible hunger through 1944, which will for ever be called Hunger Winter by those forced to go through it. Never since have I eaten tulips. Then they were part of a desperation diet.

Yet just as we had watched the German tanks roll by in 1940, then we saw the Allied tanks, with Field Marshal Montgomery in the front car, retake our city in 1945.

In 1936, moving house as a baby, all this was for the future. So was a report in *De Telegraaf*, decades later, that a house in our old street had become the most expensive in the city, when it was bought by the famous footballer, Marco van Basten.

Long after the war, when I was in my late teens, came the most profound change imaginable in my life and lifestyle, caused by a freakish twist of fate – in some ways a thunderbolt, maybe a divine intervention.

It brought about what could be called a 'heart transplant' – not literally, not a medical procedure, just something that happened deep inside and which took place in a small country of which I knew nothing.

Everything turned on its head for me. Nothing was ever the same again, the day I bought two eggs in alien Wales.

CHAPTER 1

Philosophy and Patisserie

THE HEAVY OAK front door of our new home, with its brass letterbox, had my father's name and title beautifully hand-painted thereon: Professor Herman Dooyeweerd.

It could not mention his achievements and fame. No door was ever big enough. He was our father, who we loved but not one with whom we spent much time or who was very approachable. We did not spend much time together as he was always in his study working or else travelling abroad. If we needed something important, he would arrange a time for us to come back later, a kind of appointment.

We did not realise what a marvellously talented and influential man he was until we became older; it is difficult to appreciate something that is so close to you. He was seen, when he died in 1977, as the most important philosopher in Holland's history, and was known throughout Europe. He wrote around 20 books (all totally impenetrable to us!) and an incredible number of articles and regular features in newspapers. He travelled all over the world.

I feel that I should give you a flavour of his work. Dr Paul B. Cliteur wrote in 1994:

> Herman Dooyeweerd is undoubtedly the most formidable
> Dutch philosopher of the twentieth century ... As a humanist
> I have always looked at my own tradition in search for similar
> examples. They simply don't exist. Of course, humanists
> too wrote important books, but in the case of Herman
> Dooyeweerd we are justified in speaking about a philosopher
> of international repute.

He was (and is) so important that other people wrote books about him and his philosophy and his thinking; even recently you will find new books introducing new generations to the Dooyeweerd philosophy, new societies forming to talk about him online. His 'collected works' book is still apparently selling. There is a book about 'The future of Dooyeweerd studies'.

We never pretended to enjoy his books or even to read them! For those who might be able to follow, here are two observations from key people in his field:

> He refused to take for granted that theoretical thinking is
> neutral or adequate to understand the pre-theoretical – but
> he did not react against it. This can encourage research to be
> more relevant.
>
> Dooyeweerd respected diversity and coherence more than
> most did. For example, we experience physical, biological,
> psychological, technical, social and religious aspects of life.
> And all are important.
>
> He was against both reductionism and laissez-faire
> fragmentation – and gave reasons for being so. This can make
> research findings more robust.

As a result, he delineated a suite of 15 aspects of reality, which has proven highly serviceable in practice and research. These aspects are irreducible to each other, yet form an intimate coherence of meaning, via inter-aspect dependency and analogy. Dooyeweerd's aspects have proven extremely useful in research, especially for analysis.

Dooyeweerd took meaningfulness more seriously than most philosophers do.

And the second:

He sought to discern what philosophy would, could or should be like if it were to be appropriate to helping us analyse everyday experience. To do this, he first made a longitudinal transcendental critique of the theoretical attitude of thought, which he argued is the antithesis of a pre-theoretical or everyday attitude, demonstrating that the presuppositions that either enable or hinder philosophy in viewing everyday experience are religious in nature.

Dooyeweerd himself explicitly chose a religious starting point that is different from those that have informed Western philosophy, namely those of ancient Greece, the mediaeval scholastics, and the humanist modern era; his starting point was the Biblical notion of creation, fall and redemption. As Basden (2008) explains, this starting point freed him to take seriously the diversity and coherence we experience in the everyday attitude, and that meaning is more fundamental than being.

My father founded and was editor-in-chief (1936–76) of the journal *Philosophia Reformata*. After the war he travelled extensively – to Switzerland, South Africa, France, Belgium, the United States (including several times to Harvard University) and Canada. It was the lectures during one of the tours to North America that formed the basis of

In the Twilight of Western Thought (1960), which experts believe is his best book.

Phew. As his family we never tried to make 'a longitudinal transcendental critique' of his work. Understandably. But looking back now, it is so fabulous that he was clearly a man in his element and gained so much satisfaction for all his work. In the 1940s he was also to prove more than a match for the Gestapo in the war.

He didn't really have time to take a big part in the bringing-up of nine children and, in our way, we didn't have time for him either, because we had our lives and he was completely taken over by his own work. He did have some relaxation – with his playing of the grand piano, so beautifully; and he also followed Ajax, the football team in Amsterdam. But he was following his life's call, which was fabulous, and we were always proud of him.

This is what my brother Herman Arnold wrote, lovely words:

> Father was a gifted man but in ways of a very down-to-earth
> person with his feet on the ground. We in the family loved
> him dearly and are, we think justifiably, proud of him. We
> remember him as someone who was humble before his God
> and always strove to be in his service. In the days just before
> his death I personally witnessed how he struggled greatly
> with the fact that, in his own eyes, he had not done all that he
> seemingly felt God had called him to do.

*

But was my mother any less amazing? She was an extremely clever and talented woman, she had so much about her and there were any number of areas in which she could have excelled. But she always backed him, she didn't think of putting herself first and she had decided that was how it was going to be.

And she was busy, busy, busy. She eventually had nine children, two of whom were born in the war years (we lost a tenth sibling at birth). We had a lot of students visit because of our father's work, and a lot of colleagues coming for dinner. She didn't give herself time for much else. She got on with life and was an amazing woman and looked after everybody.

Our father's large study and the room attached were not the noisiest of our house – noise of any sort was banned when he was working. This room of many memories was filled with beautiful grand and often ethnic furniture, bookcases all round, a huge bay window from which the flagpole emerged, wooden floors strewn with Persian rugs. This room was used once for a wedding reception, with the study as an overspill room. When you think that 80 people were invited to the wedding, you get an idea as to the size of the room.

My father's desk was a large oak extending table. He looked out to sliding glass doors which led to a balcony with gravel underfoot. There was one radio in my father's study, which was usually only on when he was shaving. There was a well-hidden vanity unit in one part of the study where my father would be shaving accompanied by classical music or a riveting football match!

The room on the ground floor at the front of the house was very ornate with lots of heavy antique furniture, and was only used on birthdays and other special occasions. The large sash windows looked out on a wide, tree-lined avenue.

On the ground floor there was also a large parlour, a dining room, and a sun room, all with heavy sliding doors in between. The kitchen had long granite worktops, a black-and-white patterned stone-tiled floor, a long extendable table, built-in cupboards with glass doors. In one of the three cellars was a store for the coke that fed the boiler. The boiler served radiators throughout the entire house, although the heat lost most of its momentum before reaching the upper floors.

There were marble floors throughout our vestibule and hallway. The grand flights of stairs (36 steps each) had fancy mahogany handrails, and there were high decorated ceilings and very spacious rooms.

In the hallway there hung a very musical gong which sounded like a glockenspiel. This rang every meal time. This was then followed by a rush down the stairs of all the occupants, invariably starving!

The first floor consisted of a landing, a bathroom with a marble floor, a bath on four iron feet with an enormous copper boiler for hot water. On this floor was also my father's study (no admittance without permission), with an en-suite grand piano room next to it, and sliding doors between which were never shut.

The second floor contained three large bedrooms, two double and one single, then a landing with steps leading down to another large balcony. The third floor had a landing, three bedrooms, of which one was a double, plus a large attic-room, containing a full-size table tennis table, a swing and rings which were dangling from the ceiling.

This is where lots of fun was had after school with friends. The room was later transformed into a bedsit which was rented out; it even had its own potbellied stove for heating. This was also the room where we hid people during the war, in tiny 'corridors' behind wood panelling.

The very top storey of the house was, in later years, occupied by a string of lodgers. Some were students; then there were nurses, a vicar and his wife, and a weaver, who came complete with her enormous weaving loom. The latter was hoisted all the way to the top of the house by way of 'the hook' – something that all Dutch houses of that period possessed – situated at the front gable of the house. Heavy or large pieces of furniture were thus hoisted up from the street and guided through an open window.

There was a toilet on each floor, containing an elaborately patterned cistern (also a period feature), with mahogany seats and lid, a hand wash basin with hot and cold running water, mirrors and shelves and hooks to hang one's clothes. These toilets were also used as washrooms.

The bathroom was used once a week by each member of the family, which was the norm in those days. I have to exclude my father from this, as he took a cold shower every day (under a hand shower) after exercising. The garden, which was a big one for a townhouse, was my mother's pride and joy. A gardener used to come once a year; after that my mother tended everything.

Our home was always filled with sound of music. There was a piano in the dining room, as noted the grand piano in my father's study, and another one on the third floor belonging to one of the lodgers.

At one time we had my mother's brother, Uncle Joop, lodging with us. He played the trombone. Another sound would come from upstairs, where a Jewish girl of 13 played the violin, or tried to! We all had piano lessons, and two of my older sisters became accomplished singers later in life.

It was such a beautiful house. In my young days, and if the landing door was open into the piano-room, I would be drawn by the beautiful piano music and come down and sit on the stairs and listen, vowing that one day I would also play like my father.

It was a dream unfulfilled, but how was I to know then where the path of life would lead me! Very far from the same kind of home comforts, had I but known it.

*

There were no televisions in Holland yet. I think they started to come into the shops around 1955. Not that my parents would have bought one; one made one's own entertainment! In my younger years, my sister Eveliene would appoint herself in charge of staging family plays in which we all had a part. She loved playing the piano and singing, and she would write songs for us all to perform. I remember one song was about flower fairies in a garden, and I was cast as the English rose! Well, she was almost right!

We all had bicycles to get around, so the vestibule always housed at least eight bikes. The lodgers all had their own, so the overflow was parked against the front of the house. It was a normal sight in Amsterdam as in many cities in Holland, with the lack of hills. It is still the same nowadays.

We had a series of nannies, home helps and cleaning ladies, some young, some older, quite a variety but the girls in the family also had to do their bit. After finishing school, at roughly 18, each of the girls had to do a year-long stint in housekeeping so as to be ready for marriage – at least in that department! Boys were excluded, of course! The housekeeping involved a lot of work, despite having home help as well.

One strong memory I have is of polishing the silver cutlery. You can imagine how much of it there was, with 16 people sitting down to eat at the table on many days.

My mother would instruct me on how to put the cutlery back into the drawers at the end of the job, every spoon and fork had to be carefully lined up to nestle into its neighbour (not a practice that has stayed with me at the farm!). I presume there would not be enough room for them all otherwise!

We would be earning a little pocket money during that time, so we could go to the pictures on a Saturday night for instance. We had just about enough.

The Bible was read every dinner time, some of us having our own little bibles to keep up with my father's reading. Prayers were said before every meal and churchgoing was compulsory every Sunday. I, for one, thank my father for the faith in God that I have.

Domestic services, as I would call them, were amazing in Holland at the time I lived at home. A baker would call every day on a *bakfiets* (which was a big wooden container built on the front of a bicycle), which, I am sure, was also used in this country. The wooden container had a lid, and inside were stored all the loaves of freshly-baked bread and rolls.

This man would peddle from door to door, street by street. We used to get through four loaves a day, two brown, two white. The milkman had a similar vehicle, but without the lid. It would carry two small milk churns, and on the side of these churns would be dangling two measures, one for a litre and another for half a litre.

Customers would bring a pan to the door and the milkman would measure the required amount into this pan. You can imagine the size of the pan we used to have filled.

As a child I used to feel so sorry for our old milkman. He used to take this big pan off me with big purple hands, matching his big purple nose and face, through being out in all weathers. He always wore black, fingerless gloves and a threadbare cloth cap. His eyes would be bloodshot and running with tears, whatever the weather.

The pan of milk would always go straight into the cellar to keep cool. During the summer months my mother would always boil the milk immediately, before putting it in the cellar, to stop it from going off. There were no fridges in those days.

The cellar also held a cabinet for all the dairy products, butter, eggs, cheese and meat. There was a long wooden staircase into the cellar. With all that trudging up and down the stairs and all the floors, obesity was unknown.

Another service that came to the door was the *putjesschepper*, a man carrying a small ladle, like a scoop on the end of a long metal stick, and a bucket. This was used to clean out solid waste that would accumulate in the house drain, which was situated at the back of the house. This would stop any build-up and consequent blockage of pipes feeding into the main town drains. After filling his bucket with the dregs, he would walk back through the kitchen, hall and vestibule, and into the street, leaving the most nauseating stink behind. What a job.

I remember one man talking to my mother one day, and telling her about his daughter who had contracted TB. He was collecting postage stamps to send her to a sanatorium to recover. There was a lot of TB in Holland at the time and, for people who could not pay for the treatment, there was a scheme whereby one could pay with so many postage stamps. One would have to save thousands!

And this scheme was used a lot. How that worked I have never found out but, on hearing this tragic tale, I decided to give my entire collection of stamps to this man and the album into which I had stuck them. (Stamp collecting was one of my many pastimes, as were collecting cigar bands and matchbox tops.)

Of course, there were some turbulent times during my teenage years – surely that was only to be expected. There were emotional times, lots of boyfriends, and I seemed always to be madly in love, or in the deepest despair when things went wrong.

But, at the same time, I can look back on very fulfilling and adventurous years.

I went to a private school for girls, which specialised in languages and domestic science. The rest of the subjects were like the run-of-the-mill curriculum for schools at that time.

Attending school is not included in my memories of a happy childhood, especially as mine was a girls' school which, in my opinion, does not give you a healthy outlook on members of the opposite sex.

The traditional conversations in school amongst the girls were subjects such as fashion, hairstyles, your figure, and with everything apparently edged by a general cattiness.

None of this was of any interest to me whatsoever. I

had a great girlfriend who was, like me, more interested in boys. There was a boys' school directly opposite our school. The joyous time which we both craved, and for which we could not wait, was when boys and girls would come streaming out of these two buildings and meet in a large throng.

Although I hated most of the lessons, there were two subjects I excelled in. They were anatomy and art. I am not sure of the significance of this. I finished school early, at the age of 17 – I passed my finals in every subject, except English, which I was told was a language I would never master. I worked very hard, the goal being that I was determined not to do any class twice. I was, in fact, the only one out of all nine Dooyeweerd children to pass the final exams of our school years.

In my way I had made history. I will never forget my father's great delight on hearing the news that, at last, one of his offspring had been awarded that elusive and important final certificate.

My mother promptly ordered the most amazing treat on the telephone – it was a take-away, I suppose – called *ijstaart*. It came from the best patisserie in Amsterdam.

It consisted of a base, in the shape of a bowl, made out of dark chocolate, and this was filled with Italian ice-cream, fresh fruit and topped with whipped cream. And toasted nuts. Heaven!

CHAPTER 2

Hunger Winter

No DOUBT, FOR my parents and older siblings the invasion by German forces on 10 May 1940 was desperately worrying. But I was only five when they marched into Amsterdam and the Gestapo set up their headquarters so close by. The general population was devastated; I was too young to appreciate why.

The Germans wanted air bases in Holland to use to attack Britain, and they wanted to dominate the whole area. So they invaded Belgium and Luxembourg at the same time.

Being so young, it is not so much the disturbing big picture that I remember, but the small things. Why was my mother taping all the windows in the house with brown sticky tape, in a criss-cross pattern, leaving small squares? Clearly it was done to stop glass from shattering when the bombs started to fall.

And I remember the carbite. Do they have carbite now? The Germans imposed a curfew at 8pm every evening. No lights on anywhere from that time on. All curtains had to be drawn. So no light came from any of the houses and other buildings, so as to obscure towns and cities from the 'enemy' planes.

We had a few carbite lamps in the house to give us some light because candles had long ago sold out in Amsterdam. Carbite was a crystallised substance, like small sugar lumps. Once lit, it would stay alight and the crystals were put into a lamp that looked very much like an old miner's lamp.

It also had a glass surround that would magnify the light. Once lit, I remember they gave off the most horrible fumes, like rotten eggs! We thought sometimes we'd rather be in the dark.

There were so many deeper concerns which I was too young to understand. It had been so long since our country had experienced a war. We had been neutral throughout the First World War and, while most sympathies lay solidly with Britain and the Allies, we hoped to avoid a conflagration again. It had been five generations since we had last been invaded.

Father and mother were also clearly worried about the Jewish friends that they knew, some of whom had fled Germany for Holland for their own safety. Many Jews simply committed suicide when the German invasion happened.

My mother and father were incredibly courageous throughout the occupation. They never transmitted their concern on to us younger ones, and so I don't remember feeling terrified, but they must often have been at their wits' end.

*

War had been in the air across Europe for a long time. So I learned as I grew older that the German invasion on 10 May 1940 was hardly a shock. But that evening the prime minster gave a broadcast assuring us that our armed forces would deal with the invaders, we should not worry and, in fact, there were areas in the country where our army held off the Nazis. This was true, and there must have been feats of amazing courage.

But we learned later that almost exactly half of our air force, which still included biplanes, had been destroyed on day one. And while the Germans had their Panzer divisions, we only had little tanks which they called tankettes! Our fire service comprised almost entirely of local volunteers on carts that had to be pushed.

One evening we heard huge explosions and we knew immediately that nearby Schiphol Airport was being attacked – and then Rotterdam was bombed with terrible casualties two days later. It was razed to the ground, and 30,000 people were killed. It was seen as a war crime and, suddenly, our country felt naked.

Without any air cover, and with Germany threatening to bomb Utrecht as well, the Dutch government surrendered. Queen Wilhelmina and her family had already escaped to Britain, together with the cabinet. So, a few days after we had been told that things were OK, we then heard that Holland had surrendered. It was both a shock and the only thing we could do.

I do remember bombs dropping, mostly at night – we all got up and gathered around the kitchen table. These bombs were usually still aimed at places like airports. The main one, Schiphol – named Fluegelhorns 561 by the Germans – was quite close to us, and then the Germans came in unopposed to the city and the city centre. The Gestapo set up their headquarters over the road and, worst of all, large numbers of Dutch people with Nazi leanings or Germans domiciled in Holland greeted them.

One night my mother woke us so that we could watch a burning aeroplane falling out of the sky. It came right over our house, and ended up in the park just behind. It was like a slow-motion picture.

It must be remembered that for some time the occupation was not as savage as it proved to be in other countries overrun by the Germans. Holland had declared itself neutral – although clearly supporting the Allies – and Dutch ships which escaped joined up with the British Royal Navy.

The Germans also hoped that the Dutch people might be tempted to join their National Socialism cause, and so they tried what was called a 'velvet glove' occupation – although they were always trying to round up Jews and, indeed, by the end of the war well over two-thirds of the Jewish population of the country had disappeared.

The Germans ordered that Jewish people had to wear a yellow Star of David sewn onto their sleeves to identify them. Sometimes after that they were just shot in the street. We saw that happen on the way to school.

Our people staged a general strike to protest at the persecution of the Jews, the only time action of that sort was taken in any occupied country. The ringleaders were executed as a warning.

At curfew time a siren would go off, as it did every time any planes were spotted coming our way. My father would don a helmet and armband, and with torch in hand would hurry around the block of houses where we lived, and make sure everybody was indoors. I think he must have volunteered to be a member of some kind of Home Guard or perhaps a warden.

That was my father's physical bit for the war effort and the resistance, but he did a lot more on paper to annoy the Germans. He was a prolific writer throughout his life and he wrote a weekly column in a Dutch newspaper, *De Telegraaf*, in which he spoke about all manner of things, including the occupation. He refused to stop.

My father was hauled in front of the Gestapo four times. I think the same lieutenant wanted to talk to him. You can imagine my poor mother's desperate anxiety at times like that, wondering if we would ever see him again. I suppose he was clever enough with words to be able to make his points subtly, and he also spoke fluent German, which must have impressed his interviewers – even though he did not care for the Germans at all.

There was some suggestion that what he wrote – showing such good knowledge of the war in general – made them think he must be listening to the BBC, but they were never to find his radio hidden behind his bookcase. Radios were banned.

One day they came in uniforms and my mother told them that my father was in but couldn't speak to them. They pushed her aside. They told my father they were arresting him under some accusation or other. My mother said that my father hadn't eaten all day and that there was no food in the house whatsoever. They said that if he came with them they would give him some bread. So off he went, maybe for a few hours, and they did give him bread and then he came back.

As a family we also took part in the distribution

of underground newspapers. There seemed to be an incredible number in Amsterdam, one was called *Oranje-bulletin*. They were passed around in conditions of great secrecy. My mother and one of my older sisters also did their bit by going out early in the evening on certain days delivering clandestine newspapers. These they would hide in their coats, or in their underwear.

As the Germans confiscated all radios, there was no way to find out how the war was going. Hence the clandestine newspapers. But there was one other way my parents could keep up with the news.

As noted earlier, my father managed to keep his radio while all the others were being taken away. He hid it behind a row of books in his study, where no one would look. As the war drew on, my parents would invite their neighbours to come and listen to news bulletins sent out by the BBC in the evening. These neighbours would not come in by the front door, but via a fire escape door that joined the attics (the whole row of houses was connected like that, and the doors were camouflaged by a piece of furniture so as not to be noticed). I can always remember the boom-boom of Big Ben in London while everyone gathered around, though we had to keep our distance as children, and were not sure what the gathering was for.

There was a good reason for keeping us in the dark – we were too young to understand and there was the risk that we might have shared our knowledge with others, unwittingly. I would see these people arriving in the evening and going straight to my father's study. I couldn't understand anyway and it was all in English.

Schools still operated for a while, but they were also in the hands of the Germans. I attended a primary school and there was a big picture of the Queen of Holland hanging in the entrance hall.

That was ripped down by the Germans and replaced by a huge portrait of Hermann Göring. He was the creator of the Gestapo and then head of the Luftwaffe. A gracious portrait was replaced by the image of a fat bully.

Gradually the 'velvet glove' approach ended and life became far more tough and frightening. Jews were rounded up and sent to labour camps and the death camps, like Auschwitz, where they were stripped of everything. A family opposite us disappeared and were never seen again. I remember the sadness in our house and my mother looking so worried.

There were lots of good Dutch people who hid Jews from the Germans, like my parents did. We took in a Jewish lady and her 13-year-old daughter. We were told they were distant members of our family. If anyone asked, they were supposed to be our Aunty Ilse and Marianne, her daughter.

We (the smaller children in the family) never questioned that. It would have been very dangerous to have told us the truth, as German soldiers often accompanied children on their way home from school, and questioned them about all sort of things. They would be friendly, making jokes, but they were also looking for information: who was hiding people and where, and they were serious about obtaining it.

I was once escorted in that way, and you can imagine my mother's anguish on opening the front door and seeing me standing between two German soldiers. I obviously did not spill the beans about this brand-new aunty we had suddenly acquired. 'Aunty' Ilse's husband had already been taken away by the Germans, and was never heard of again.

At the start the Germans were reasonably friendly. They sent propaganda photographs back to Germany which appeared to show soldiers chatting amiably with locals. But it was all a sham. Gradually things became worse; the invaders became more and more desperate for labour to keep their occupation going. Young men were rounded up all over Amsterdam to work in labour camps. They would come round the houses knocking on the doors and searching.

Again, unbeknown to us younger siblings at the time, we had another hiding place. There were wooden panelled walls in the attic, behind which was a long passage about two feet wide.

Every house in our avenue had a fire escape door on the top floor, connecting with the attic of the next house via this passage. Very handy at that time because all the boltholes effectively had two different exits.

These three lads slept in there at night, in case of a raid by the Germans, and hid in there at times during the day when the Germans were doing 'house calls'. If anyone had discovered any of our guests, the future could have been awful for us all.

*

Real problems started to arise when the shops ran out of food and 1944 was terrible. It is still referred, to this day, as the *Hongerwinter* (hunger winter). It had become clear for some time that the invaders wanted to starve Amsterdam, which in many ways became a ghost town, with people dying of hunger often when their children had been sent away.

Amsterdam was surrounded and besieged. Nothing came in, and what did get through was immediately confiscated by the Germans. Shops closed. 'Soup kitchens' started to appear, and long lines of people started to form every day to get some of the 'food' on offer. (Pig swill would have been a better name for it, but at least it was something to keep us going.)

The 'menu' was varied. One day it would be bread pudding, consisting of lumps of some sort of bread boiled in water with a bit of milk powder added. The next day one could collect a quantity of beetroot chunks boiled in water.

One had to bring a pan and hope you would make it home without spilling any, the pan being placed on the saddle of the bike. We all took turns in fetching the food on offer and ate every scrap of it.

Some people could not get to these soup kitchens and made their own survival food, like boiling up tulip bulbs in water and making soup out of nettles. The citizens of Amsterdam were starving and people started dying. I remember vividly a man coming to our front door begging for food. As I ran to the kitchen to ask my mother, I heard a slump behind me where this poor man had actually dropped down dead.

This was the time that my mother made up her mind that the younger children would have to leave Amsterdam and go to farms in the countryside if they were to survive. She was given a few addresses by a group of people who helped to organize this, the thinking being that there would always be food on the farms.

So off we went, first by train, the rest of the route we each walked carrying a kind of wicker suitcase (which were widely used in those days) with a strap around it.

My older brother Herman went first and ended up on a farm where he stayed till the end of the war. My younger sister Freddie and I went to the same farm to start with but were separated a little later, which was very hard. My older sister Eveliene also went to stay on yet another farm.

I remember the one farm where we stayed. We slept in a lovely cosy bed that was in a sort of cupboard next to the chimney breast. There was a thick curtain to pull across the opening and we felt like we were in our own little nest.

One evening, I heard the farmer in the living room and decided to peek out through my curtain to see what was going on. I was a very curious child. To my horror, I saw him sitting on the edge of his chair by the fire, using the bread knife to trim some particularly thick and coarse toenails. Absolute fascination for a small child! I don't remember it putting me off the bread the next day, though!

When we first arrived, my sister Freddie and I were, of course, desperately thin. The farmer and his wife took one look at us and resolved to make us fit and healthy again. So the next morning, at breakfast, they proudly presented us with a glass each of colostrum from the farm cows, to build us up and get us strong. The colostrum is the first milk that the cow produces for its calf, and it contains antibodies and stacks of nutrients.

It is also thick and yellowish. We had to drink it but, oh, it was so horrible! We had this to look forward to every morning for a while. But those people did their best for us and I have been extremely strong and healthy all my life. So maybe the colostrum is the secret.

In those days, all the farms had huge heavy horses to pull the ploughs and various carts, depending on the task. One summer at the farm, we were playing outside where the farm lads were working, and one of them offered me a chance to sit on the back of one of these enormous horses.

I imagined how exciting it would be, so I agreed. Once I was on board, however, the lad gave the horse a whack across its broad rump and it took off, galloping across the field with me hanging on for dear life. That memory stays with me even now as one of my most frightening experiences. I think the farm boys were just having a bit of fun, but of course it was very different for a skinny little child straight out of Amsterdam.

Very soon I was on my third hosting farm, somewhere on an island in the very north of Holland. When the tide came in you could only get off this place by rowing boat. I got very homesick there as the farmer's daughter, who was much older than me, used to bully me and shut me in a little attic-room for long periods. I was told not to say a word about this, and to do as I was told. It made me very unhappy.

During the time we were on the first two farms my mother would come all the way from Amsterdam on her pushbike. It had solid tyres. There were no rubber blow-up tyres available, as the Germans were stopping people on bikes and commandeering them. But we had so many that at least we kept one or two.

The ride for my mother, with those solid tyres, was incredibly uncomfortable. She would cycle for well over

34

three hours to where I was staying, and the farmer's wife would give her some good food to eat from the farm, such as potatoes with melted butter (their own). The problem was that my poor mother did not get food like that in Amsterdam; her system was not used to it. So consequently she suffered dreadful tummy pains and diarrhoea. There was also an occasion where my mother cycled to the farm and all the way home with a bag of potatoes, only to have them taken away by the Germans on her return.

Then came the winter of 1944. Hundreds of Amsterdam's people died from the cold and starvation. I remember my mother still coming to see us occasionally, exhausted and hollow-eyed and stick thin under her long coat.

She would always return to Amsterdam with a metal container of milk for the new baby – Joop, my younger brother, who was born in that dreadful year. Sometimes she would also be given a small bag of potatoes, which would be strapped onto her back. Ilse, the Jewish lady we had taken in, looked after Joop when my mother was away.

On one of the long treks home after a farm visit, she was caught in a snowstorm, fell off her bike and banged her head, and lost consciousness. By the grace of God, she was found very soon by a doctor, who was in his car in the area. He took her all the way home, and she survived the whole ordeal.

There was no fuel to be had in Amsterdam and people had already begun to cut down trees. All the huge trees in our avenue were cut down and used for fuel. There was no electricity either, so after dark the horrible old carbite lamps came out. My father continued his book writing throughout the war, using a precious candle when the light was fading. There was always a candle for him, of course.

Wherever we were during the war years, we had to go to school. Schools in Amsterdam were all closed and taken over by the Germans. As city children having to attend country schools, it wasn't easy. There was many a tearful day. We were called names and generally bullied.

From one farm we used to walk there and back to school, nearly two miles. But on a Tuesday there was a market, and on that day we had a ride in the horse and cart one way at least.

On the whole, my stay at the different farms left me with good memories, especially the spell when my sister and I stayed together. When staying on my own the old homesickness would come back now and again.

At some point during the war years my older sister Mieke went to Friesland, a province in the north of Holland, to stay with relations. She was then 18 years of age. She was unable to come back to Amsterdam for a long time because there was no public transport connection back to the city.

She met a local doctor called Magnus Zeebrugge there. They fell in love and got married without my parents knowing anything about it. There were no communications between Amsterdam and the rest of the country, no telephone calls coming in and no telegrams.

When she eventually came home, via horse and cart and maybe the odd tram, she took everyone completely by surprise by revealing her new husband. My mother, despite all the privations, despite the Hunger Winter, insisted on having the whole wedding party again. So members of the family who lived relatively close by, and who were able to come on foot or cycle, were summoned to come and celebrate!

I had a lot of uncles and aunts, obviously. My mother walked miles and miles around the relations, asking for any scrap of food, anything. 'We're having a wedding, so come and join us.'

There was, of course, hardly any food to go round but, somehow, most of them brought something, whatever they could get hold of. There was a black market in Amsterdam, where a few items of food could be had at an extortionate price. There were also some cigarettes on sale. You went and bought at your own risk.

There is a photo of the whole wedding party, where everybody looks like ghosts from another planet, haunting and pale. Everyone had black rings around their eyes from malnutrition. My mother had gone down in weight to just six stone, and my grandmother weighed even less. Both were tall, well-built women before that terrible time.

The other common feature of the war was head lice. They were an epidemic. During the war years everybody was infested with head lice, old and young. No wonder; bad food, if any, with immunity very low and conditions dreadful. My mother would take the girls with long hair (mine was long, thick and curly) into the bathroom, armed with one of those awful 'nit combs'. She would struggle through our tangled hair. With heads bowed over the wash basin, one by one the little critters would tumble out. It was a screaming time; the tugging was so painful!

After that was over, we would don a turban made out of old clean nappies. This was drenched in vinegar to kill any remaining lice eggs, according to my mother.

Because we scratched our heads all day, we had some open little scabs. You can imagine the stinging!

The next day we would smell very vinegary, because it was just washed off, that was all. No shampoo to be had of course. There were also no other toiletries, like soap or toilet paper. There was a kind of soap one could get. It resembled a block of hard clay, with a light green colour. I remember it as feeling gritty, no scent and resulting in some sort of foam that died straight away. But, like everything else, better than nothing.

We heard in snippets that the war was going badly for Germany, and that the Allies were gaining the upper hand which was joyous to hear. Rumours had been growing for some time that the Germans were capitulating, and that freedom was not far away. The Germans in the Gestapo building opposite our house were getting nervous and jumpy, so too German soldiers.

Marja, my sister, was very fond of a man who came to our house, not to see my father about learned matters, but about painting. He earned his living from painting and did beautiful paintings in oils throughout the war. Often he did copies of the work of Rembrandt, not as a fraud but because he loved the style. We had one of his works at home.

The relationship grew. Although we always had a house full of people, with so little food for them all, my mother allowed Marja's friend and his two brothers to hide with us.

We, as younger children, were not supposed to know this because they were hidden in the top of our house and they were very thankful to my mother for what she'd done for them. The Germans were watching from the big house opposite.

Marja's painter man was one of those that the Germans had their eyes on. We didn't know exactly why. To this day I haven't got a clue. He stayed safe, but they did not end up together.

On one evening, just before the British and Canadian tanks rolled into Amsterdam, we had a visit from two very drunk Gestapo men looking for three men they claimed to have seen on the roof of our house. Being so sure that freedom was on its way, our hidden men got very cocky, and climbed through the attic window onto the roof, to see what was happening in the streets below.

The German soldiers rang the doorbell, and for once 'Aunty' Ilse opened the door. (She was never allowed to do this in case her very Jewish appearance would give her away.)

But they went straight past her, and ordered both my parents into the garden at gunpoint, and asked a lot of questions about the sighting of these men on the roof.

Mieke took us towards the top of the house for safety, and we looked down and saw that they had mother and father at gunpoint and were cocking their rifles.

Not satisfied with the answers they got, they went into every room in the house looking for the lads. I remember so well that, at the time, I was on the toilet on the second floor. My mother, in the meantime, had ran upstairs and hammered on the toilet door. 'Hurry up... hurry up!' she shouted. 'Let me in!' She had newspapers in her hand, one of the underground publications similar to the ones she used to deliver in the evenings. She then started to frantically rip them up and flushed them down the loo.

It was very close to the last day of the war and the Germans seemed as nervous as we did. In the end quite a few of the Germans left it too late to escape and they were captured.

In the meantime, the three men had quickly climbed back down from the roof. Two of them crept back to their hideout, but my sister's boyfriend had called in at her bedroom, and was not able to make it back to the hideout.

Hearing the Germans coming up the stairs, he quickly got into the bed. My mother had seen the whole thing happen and promptly stood guard in front of the bedroom door, telling the Germans that there was somebody in that room who was seriously ill with a contagious disease – knowing that the Germans were always scared of catching anything at that time, when there was so much disease around.

So they eventually left, not before one last cruel act. They took a piece of bacon, which was given to my mother on her last trek to the farm where I had stayed. She had hidden it in the wardrobe of her bedroom, and the Germans came across it and took it. The fact that they were drunk was probably our saving, especially for my parents. They were in bitter mood.

The next day tanks came rolling down our avenue. It was 5 May; they were friendly tanks, with British, Canadian and Polish soldiers. It was incredibly exciting, and for our parents and for our city indescribably joyous. The dark clouds had lifted.

Some of our family stood on the balcony at the front of the house, and I remember my father pointing out Field Marshal Montgomery to me. He was standing up at the front of a military jeep, big cigar and all.

The jubilation was ear-shattering. Everybody ran out

into the streets, including the Dooyeweerd family, all pushing forward to get as close as possible to our heroes. I was still only nine, and remember how high the side of the tanks looked, and the terrific clattering noise they made.

We could still see the odd German rushing out of the Gestapo building in confusion. All the people came pouring out of their houses, shouting and singing. It was really amazing. The whole mob of people grew from street to street, everybody laughing, crying and shouting with excitement. People hugging and kissing each other. My brother-in-law, Magnus, sat me on his shoulders and danced around, as did my mother and everybody else.

It was such an incredible relief, though the food shortages were still with us. They opened some kitchens in the centre of Amsterdam, organised by a group of ladies. If you still had a pan, you could take it and they would pour in this terrible stuff made out of water and beetroot. You'd take back the pan on the seat of your bike. Others were still eating tulips.

There was a soup kitchen like that every day for a while. Then, I think, they were eating worms from the garden boiled in a bit of water. So we ate anything, we didn't care at all. Eventually some rationing came in and very slowly foodstuffs reappeared.

*

After some time celebrating the arrival of the friendly troops, we walked back home through the crowds and there, sitting on the doorstep all alone, was my brother Herman, a lost little soul. He had made his own way home from the farm where he had stayed, hitching a lift – a little boy of eleven years old.

As there were no communications with the world outside Amsterdam, nobody could have known that the liberation was actually happening, although it was on the cards. Herman had obviously heard talk of it at the farm where he stayed and thought he would go and look for himself. So, somehow, he managed to travel home.

When there was no-one to greet him, he assumed that everyone had died. He sat down outside the house and wept. At the time, after we had been reunited, it was just laughed off. But the memory has stayed with him to this day, a belief that he had been forgotten. However, it did not stop him in later life becoming a director of the World Bank.

In the wake of the Germans we were starving. But we were alive, and free.

CHAPTER 3

The Man
at the Door

MY ELDER SISTER Marja had one ambition as she went through her teenage years. She had her heart set on a career as an air stewardess with KLM, Royal Dutch Airlines. She decided that she should improve her English.

She left for Britain at 19 and found a job at Liberty department store on Great Marlborough Street. One day she was asked to take a parcel to an address in Soho. She lost her way and asked a London bobby, who was actually on traffic duty at the time, to help her out.

On seeing the address where she had to go, he telephoned his station and asked for a replacement to direct the traffic so he could escort Marja to her destination.

This kindly policeman, John Davies, later became her husband. He was originally from the Rhondda Valley in south Wales, though had moved up to London to join the Metropolitan Police. By 1954, when I was 18, John and Marja had returned from London and had settled in Pontnewydd (now part of Cwmbran) in Wales. Marja was pregnant with twins and, as my father said I needed to learn English too, it was arranged that I was to go to Wales to help my sister.

It was a huge adventure, and so different. I took a boat train from the Hoek van Holland to Harwich and took the train to London. I first stayed with a colleague of my father, Professor Friedman, who worked at a university in London. I stayed with him for a few days to see a bit of London.

Unfortunately, nobody could come with me as a guide, as the children were away at school and Mrs Friedman off to a meeting. But the kind Professor Friedman gave me a lift in his car to the British Museum. Oh, what joy!

He promised to pick me up again later in the afternoon after finishing his morning and afternoon lectures. It was a stifling hot day and, after a few happy hours admiring Britain's past, I went outside to sit on the steps of this huge building. I saw an ice-cream van nearby, bought myself a nice big one and returned to my place on the steps.

Whilst I sat enjoying my ice-cream, a man came up the steps and sat next to me. He said he had followed me around in the museum and said he was interested in me. He told me his name, Kenneth Goodall, and told me he was on holiday and also staying in London.

He seemed very polite, wore a suit and tie (which I found a bit strange as it was so hot!) and kept asking me questions, most of which I did not understand as my English was desperately bad. It was the one language I was no good at in school.

Just then, the professor turned up and came to my rescue. That was that… or so I thought. The next day I took the train to a town called Newport in Wales, where I was met by PC John Davies. And who should get off the train at the same station, just behind me? This man had followed me everywhere and knew where I was heading. I must have mentioned something about going to Newport when we spoke the day before, but even so... it was all very strange.

He was working in Kenya, he told me, and had to go back there within the next few days as his holiday was up. He picked me up from Marja's to go to the pictures one evening before going back to London. He tried to persuade me to go back with him to London to see him off at Heathrow, but of course that did not happen.

I did get a telegram from him the day he left for Kenya, which read: 'Vous avez perdu le bateau, n'est pas!' It was signed K. Goodall, Kenya Secret Police. Oh well. In a way I was impressed, though in later life I wondered what sort of secret policeman tells you he is a secret policeman.

I stayed with Marja and John for three months.

One day there was a knock on the door. There were two men standing there. One was a friend of John's. The other was a rather scruffy and dishevelled tall man with jet black hair and a tanned outdoor face. His name was Robert Francis. Oh boy, was he handsome! He had a tray of eggs and told me that he was selling them. I decided to buy two, just in case.

We clicked immediately, despite my English being so poor. There and then he asked me out for the following day, as he put it, 'to see a bit of Wales'. I was 18 at the time. The good-looking Welshman with the eggs was 33.

His parents were living in Caerleon. They had three children, Mary, Seymour and my good-looking Welshman, Robert, who was a farmer. He had also played rugby for Welsh Schools. At the time this was not particularly noteworthy. But when I had lived in Wales for a few years, I realised it was very big indeed. Seymour was a representative for the famous Yardley cosmetics company. Bob, as he quickly became when we met next day, had served in the Army during the Second World War, and had become a sergeant in his teens, taking part in the Battle of Monte Cassino and the release of Italy. He had served his country for eight years and was now back in Wales trying to earn some sort of living at a tough time.

We fell in love that day. Our romance blossomed and Bob took me to see his farm, called Glebe Farm, which consisted of 40 acres, on which he kept 15 milking cows, a few chickens, a horse and one pig.

The farmhouse was in a tiny village. Mamheilad is a small farming community on the very eastern edge of the south Wales coalfield. Bob's place was very old. I remember it being very dark and smelling musty, a bit like an old church. It was called Glebe Farm then, but originally 'Persondy', a name it reverted to later.

Bob had two friends living with him, Trevor and Elizabeth Moseley. They lived there for free in exchange for doing the cooking and cleaning for him. They had a little three-year-old girl called Jane. The kitchen was used as the main area where the four of them lived. There was an old Rayburn which was fuelled with coal and wood, causing lots of smoke that should have gone up the chimney, but some of it instead came back into the kitchen giving off a sulphur-like smell, which I later found out was due to a blocked chimney. There were no curtains to be seen.

Anyway, none of these things mattered to me. I was so in love with Bob, I loved everything I saw. Bob used to come every evening after milking to take me out to 'see a bit more of Wales'. Then, one day – still well within a week of meeting – he suggested a drive to the seaside and an afternoon on the beach.

So we went to a place near Barry in south Wales, where Bob proposed! We were both so very happy. Ecstatic. I could not describe it in words. We had known each other for only a few days.

That evening, I rang home to Amsterdam. I just wanted to tell the world. My parents were not amused in the least by the news, nor were Marja and John. My mother told me in no uncertain terms that I was to come home at the end of August [1954] as planned. They all mistrusted the quick timing, and the difference in our backgrounds. Not that Bob and I felt any of that.

Not long after, Marja had her babies, her twins of which one died at birth. It was a very, very sad and traumatic time. I helped as much as I could, especially with looking after Hughie, their two-year-old boy. Every evening Bob still turned up to take me away from the gloomy atmosphere. It was fine by Marja and John, who probably also wanted a bit of time on their own.

But August was looming and I had to go home. We both dreaded it. I suppose some people might think – many locals clearly did too – it was all too quick. But to us it just felt right, totally right. Bob's car was falling to pieces but he borrowed a slightly more dependable car and drove me all the way up to London and across to Harwich, an epic trip for him. There was no M4 in those days and definitely no Severn Bridge.

It was a night boat but there were no cabins available. I should have booked, of course. I spent the night on the top deck behind one of the huge chimneys, where it was a bit more sheltered and also a bit warmer. The reason why I went on the top deck and not inside was that people were being seasick everywhere as it was a very stormy night. Inside people were hanging around toilets and wash basins vomiting. It did not seem that stabilisers had been invented.

Our goodbye had been awful, and very tearful, especially because we had no idea when we would see each other again. Bob gave me a jumper to keep me warm on the boat. That came in so handy that night, although I was almost lost and drowned in it.

I slept for weeks with this jumper under my pillow, from which Bob's farm's smell was still oozing through strongly – what bliss!

My mother met me at Hoek van Holland and was astonished at my dirty and smelly appearance and wanted to know where, oh where, I had got that jumper from.

*

Bob and I corresponded from then on in. I was receiving two to three letters per week. I still have most of Bob's letters to this day, kept in an old biscuit tin to keep the paper-weevils out. They are such romantic letters. The distance between us and the differences between us were huge but there was never a time when we despaired of things.

After what seemed a lifetime, Bob came over the following February [1955] for a week. He was not to prove a great traveller in later life; he loved his home base. But he had driven all the way to Harwich again and made the crossing. In that week we were officially engaged. My mother seemed to have got over the jumper incident.

Bob first had to have a session with my father in his study. I was not allowed to be in on the conversation. Or even in the room, which was very odd.

Bob was amazed at our formality, attitudes and the furnishings in our house. It was as complete a culture shock for him as it was for me when I first visited Glebe Farm. And at the end of the meeting my parents announced that Bob and I were now engaged. I never found out what was said at the meeting.

But my mother became very fond of Bob during the week he spent with us. He brought coke up from one of the cellars for the enormous boiler which stood in the kitchen and served the central heating all over the whole house keeping the large kitchen warm also. Every evening Bob would make sure that a new scuttle of coke was brought up from the cellar so as to save my mother a heavy job. No wonder she loved him.

My father on the other hand... They had nothing in common whatsoever and my father could not understand what I wanted with a farmer. He used to tell me that he was 'not sure about your farmer'. He said that more than once.

As the week drew to a close, Bob packed for home, to go back to his farm which had been looked after by Trevor and Tom. (Tom Wheeler worked for Bob until I arrived.) I was totally inconsolable. My world had caved in.

And what now? We both wrote letters straight away, and I could tell that Bob was also desolate and down. We just wanted to be together for ever. We corresponded non-stop and all we wanted was to get married as soon as possible.

In the meantime, my mother found me a little part-time job four evenings per week (to distract me from thinking about Bob).

Bob again wrote to my father and asked for his permission to marry his daughter, a letter I never saw in which he wrote about his financial position, livestock and dead stock, and also that he would look after me and keep me in the way to which I was accustomed. We laughed about that promise for years afterwards, especially when coming in late in the evening covered in cow muck and mud!

But Bob did not get a reply to his carefully-worded letter, and wrote to me that he was very worried. My father's lack of response was worrying indeed. He was never an expressive character but this was too much. My father was not a man I could argue or plead with, and I was desperately worried that he would ignore or refuse Bob's request.

So, the plan was now that I should go to my father to ask for my own hand, so to speak. After reading Bob's letter to me, I immediately went to my father's study, knocked on the door and asked if I could speak with him. The answer was yes, tonight after dinner. The time dragged so slowly as I tried to think of a reasonable way to ask if I could marry a man I had just met, at a location where I had only been once, to move from a *herenhuis* of six floors to a tiny farm in a foreign country.

He relented. And so, it came to pass that I was given a date which suited my father, which was 22 July 1955. Bob's letter was never mentioned again. I remember seeing it on my father's desk but I thought it best to leave well alone. I had my wedding date; that was all that mattered to us.

As she was about to gain Bob as a son-in-law, my mother decided she should have a look at this Glebe Farm. My father agreed (his permission was obtained for my mother to be away, which was a major thing!) and my mother and I went over the following April to stay for a few days. I held my breath.

My father did not like my mother to be away, as she was always in charge of the whole household, making sure everything ran like clockwork. My father's world was in his study, where he spent every day, apart from giving lectures.

My mother and I could obviously not stay at the Glebe, as Trevor, Liz and little Jane were living with Bob. So it was arranged that my mother and I would stay a few nights with Mary, Bob's sister, and the rest of the time with Bob's brother Seymour and his wife Betty.

They had beautiful homes and my mother was so impressed with my future in-laws and their surroundings. She was mysteriously quiet about the ramshackle farmhouse, however. I found out later that poor Liz had spring-cleaned the whole place as best she could in preparation for my mother's visit.

Then we went back home, for me a forlorn trip. After that, time seemed to drag horribly. Bob and I were missing each other so, so much. So it was back to letter writing again.

But now there were days to tick off in the calendar. We knew the date when we would be together. It all caused a sensation amongst my family and friends, and everyone who knew the family.

It was sensational for me, too. In a lovely way.

CHAPTER 4

Carriages for Queen Hanny

WISHING SO FERVENTLY that the day would come did not make it come any quicker. But eventually 22 July came crawling round. Wedding day. Maybe people were still wondering how our paths had even crossed, let alone that we had fallen in love.

Bob had arrived the night before from Hoek van Holland after the long, long trip. He had perspiration on his forehead but was also looking very striking with his outdoor tan, black hair and those blue, blue eyes.

Together with his sister Mary and his sister-in-law, they had travelled by boat from Harwich. Neither of their husbands came; they were holding out because they thought the wedding was not appropriate and too soon. 'It'll never last!' they said.

We went to meet them at Amsterdam's Central Station and we travelled the rest of the way to my parents' house by tram. Bob and I held hands all the way and we could not stop looking at each other.

My mother opened the front door and made everyone

so welcome. Then came a very awkward moment when my mother showed Mary and Betty their bedroom, upon which Betty enquired where Bob was to sleep. 'One floor below your bedroom,' was the reply. A gasp from the two ladies. 'But Mrs Dooyeweerd, Robert is not allowed to stay under the same roof as the bride. That is the British custom if not the Dutch custom!'

My mother mumbled something and assured our two guests that she would find alternative accommodation. So she telephoned the parents of my girlfriend (this was at approximately 11 at night) to see if they could help out.

'Of course we will,' was the reply, and so Bob and I trundled over there with his case through the dimly-lit streets to where they lived, a walk of roughly 30 minutes. We did not mind in the least of course, as it gave us a chance for some long-awaited kissing and cuddling.

At six in the morning I woke my sister Fred and my girlfriend Jolke, who were to be my bridesmaids. We had put our clothes ready the day before. So after a quick dip in the bath we got dressed. I smoked cigarettes in those days and so did my girlfriend.

So we shared a few with a cup of tea. Then my mother came into the room and inspected us from head to toe.

My wonderful mother had not only made my wedding dress but also those of the bridesmaids. She had done an incredible job, everything was perfect. She had a quick cup of tea with us and left to dress herself.

The wedding carriages were due and came clopping up at 7.30 that morning, after picking Bob up from my girlfriend's house, together with her parents, who were going to be our witnesses.

We had quite a procession. We had four carriages

with a team of horses for each one plus coachmen and footmen, the latter standing on the back of each carriage. The morning of the wedding was a beautiful one – blue, blue sky, and very warm. We were in the middle of a heat wave at the time. At 7.30 I duly heard the trotting hooves of horses. It made my heart beat incredibly quickly. My veil and train were adjusted, and I made my way downstairs where our beautiful bouquets were waiting, as were all the family – my grandmother, aunts and uncles. I really did feel like a queen, and I had such a job not to burst out laughing as my two naughty bridesmaids kept on whispering witty remarks. Good job really, it stopped my trembling.

One of my father's treasured rugs was spread out on the pavement so that my dress and train would not get soiled. Then the carriage door was opened by a footman, who was dressed in full regalia.

Bob looked magnificent but slightly uneasy in his morning suit, and there were once again beads of sweat on his forehead. Both Mary and Betty were speechless; they were so impressed with all the happenings of that day.

Apparently there had been a panic, as the morning suit with tails that Bob had hired in Cardiff was too big for him. Being Bob, he had never thought to try it on before he came over.

But the mother of a friend of mine came to the rescue with a few safety pins, cleverly hidden behind his tails. His waistcoat was grey, and the envy of all the male members of my family whose hats and waistcoats were black.

So, after all the family had taken their places in the other three carriages, off we all trotted. We made a long detour in the beautiful Vondelpark, which looked wonderful at that time of year. Then we drove right through to the centre of Amsterdam to where the registry office was located.

It was a real procession. We came across scores of busy people on their way to work (as it was a Friday). They were stopping to let us through and waving; there were beaming people everywhere, and I had the biggest smile of all. I sat forward on this little hard carriage seat to wave back at them all. I had a ball, I felt like royalty again – whilst Bob sank further and further back into his seat. The high profile was not for him, that day or any other.

After the registry office ceremony concluded, we climbed back into the carriages and set off to the church where my mother had organised coffee and cake in the vestry, just for a little interval.

The minister was an army chaplain, a good friend of my parents. He always preached in his uniform. He did a sermon first in Dutch and then in English, especially for our English and Welsh guests.

After the church service we all trotted home where caterers had arranged a beautiful lunch, all set out on long tables in the living and dining rooms and going over into the sunroom, from which steps led down to the garden.

Garden furniture was put at the end of it under the trees, shielded from the hot sun.

It was so, so hot. The guests all helped themselves to food and chatted animatedly.

All the doors and windows were open, also the French windows which led onto his balcony overlooking the garden. A few of the guests stood there to catch a little of the breeze. Everywhere, there were beautiful flower arrangements.

Two surprise guests came up to us and this shook me to

the core. They were the farmer and his wife (who seemed much older than I remembered them) where I had stayed during the war when I was about seven years old. I had never forgotten her face and his slow and musical voice. It was an amazing surprise. My mother had sent them an invitation, the typical thing that my mother would do. It was all like a dream.

Drinks were served at 5.30pm. Everybody was ushered downstairs to have dinner. The caterers, again under strict instructions from my mother, had made a beautiful job of the tables and the meal. Speeches were made by my father and my uncle, who had a better knowledge of everyday English. Then glasses were raised.

Afterwards Bob and I had to hastily make our excuses and go upstairs to change. A taxi came to take us to Schiphol Airport. Bob had cows to milk!

We said our goodbyes and waved from the taxi. I had a few tears suddenly. There was so much emotion that day. I had the man I loved so much there, with his arms around me. I took my bouquet of Aaron lilies and gypsophila back with me to Wales. It had indeed been perfection, an incredible day.

Bob and I flew from Schiphol to London on a tiny aircraft. It was the first flight either of us had taken. We arrived quite late in the evening, and took a taxi into London that brought us to the Strand Palace Hotel. I was amazed at the size of the place, and inside a certain sense of grandeur met us.

We were soon checked in and shown our room upstairs. The corridor seemed endless, with red, blue and green carpet the whole length.

We followed the man with our suitcases and arrived at

our room. Oh dear. Not very welcoming. There was one light bulb in the middle of the ceiling and everything in the room was a brown and ochre-yellow colour. Awful.

Never mind, we had each other and nothing else really mattered. It was very late anyway, and we had to be up very early in the morning to catch the milk train – as it was called in those days – to Wales, my adoptive country.

Our good friend Trevor was seeing to the milking all the time Bob was away, but he had to get to his own job in Newport. So we were back to do the milking – even though at the time I had hardly ever seen a cow, even from a distance.

The sun shone brighter as we arrived back at Glebe Farm. We had a quick cuppa with Trevor before he left and we were finally on our own in our own place. Indeed, this was the place where we would stay all our lives.

I was examining the place for the first time, because previous visits had been fleeting. I looked around the kitchen for the very first time really, at a place which had seemed in my dreams so beautiful.

The reality was different. I found out that Trevor and Liz owned almost everything in the house and were taking them to their own place – things such as furniture, the bed, and the carpet in the kitchen (the living room only had a bit of a rug on the flagstone floor, which was crumbling in many places).

There was some china, odd bits and pieces including one saucepan and a frying pan. We only had a few things for wedding presents, on purpose, as we would have to carry them all the way back to Wales.

My aunts had given us a set of cutlery which we brought with us in our suitcases.

We were also given some bed linen, but no towels, too bulky. I found two towels on a shelf upstairs. What luck! Maybe if I was older I might have despaired, but I was young and in love and everything was a wonderful adventure and a challenge to rise to. I loved it.

My parents gave me 50 Dutch Guilders to buy a sewing machine. This was my mother's practical thinking again. She had noticed on her visit here that there were no curtains anywhere in the house, except in the kitchen where Trev, Liz and Bob lived. Bob told me that, really, nobody went into the living room. The kitchen was nice and warm because of the Rayburn.

It was the time to be practical. We had no curtains and I had a beautiful wedding dress. Sewing some curtains was going to be one of my first jobs, once I got the hang of life there a little. So I cut up my wedding dress. It had a full skirt and would make some pretty bedroom curtains and brighten the place up a bit, at least upstairs.

A pantry is, to this day, one of the best things to have in a house. Especially a house like ours which had no cupboards anywhere to keep things like food and general housekeeping. The pantry had a 'cold slab', as it was called, on which to keep food cold.

It all took some getting used to. There was a tiny little shop just down the road from where one could buy a few basic essentials like bacon, flour, sugar, butter, and Camp coffee. The latter was the most vile dark brown concoction (just like gravy browning), made entirely of chicory, not one coffee bean in the mix. One was supposed to use one teaspoon in a mug and top it up with hot milk. Ghastly. The Dutch are superb at coffee – I found that the Welsh were certainly not!

Mrs Davies, the owner of this little shop, sold me one more vital product, cigarettes. One could buy a full pack of 20, a half-pack, or just a couple in a paper bag.

My wedding bouquet was still in quite good shape, so I decided to hang it on the partition in the spare room, and that's where it stayed for years.

That must have been the start of my love for dried flowers, as many years later I grew lots of flowers to be dried in my veg patch. As for the rest of the spare room – there was hardly anything there; the floor was uneven, freezing cold in the winter, and only floorboards between the downstairs rooms and the first floor. There was nothing else there to form a ceiling.

People always ask me what I was feeling when I woke up after my first night at the farm in this totally different culture, out in the country, not in the city that I knew and really loved. I had landed in a place where I could not speak the language and where I was surrounded not by my large family any more but by cows and a pig, and the all-pervading smell – in a house which had curtains because I had cut up my gorgeous wedding dress. People still occasionally ask me the same questions, 64 years on.

People also wondered what my lovely mother thought. Did she worry about me? Well, she would never say if she did. She was like that always, she would not really talk to any of the children about things that were more private for her.

I never had heart-to-heart sessions with my mother at all. She just got on with life and looked after everybody and she was an amazing woman. Once you got married or you moved away from home, these things hit you, because I did miss her in the beginning, just really asking about things, normal things after you got married. I did only know Bob for a month in total; then hardly saw him till the wedding. And then I discovered that he only took one bath per year...

And of course, in those days it was a long journey and it was not easy to stay in touch, even by telephone. If I had been truly desperate to make a telephone call to Bob before the wedding, I pressed my father, and if he said yes then he reminded me that he was monitoring the time as it was so expensive.

And there is significance in that I retained my Dutch passport and citizenship. I never held a British passport and so could not even vote in parliamentary elections. To obtain a British passport in those years would have cost five shillings!

But I never had a second's regret, not in all those years that I spent with Bob. We spent so much time together, sometimes almost every minute of the day, partly because Bob never really wanted to go out. I used to say that he would build a moat around the place if he could. We were so happy together.

After the first night we spent together in our house, I woke to see Bob standing over me with a cup of tea on a tray. Also on this little tray stood a tumbler, containing a single red rose, picked from our garden. So romantic!

As it turned out, that was the one and only time that it happened, but it was so lovely. One crazy journey had just ended, another was just beginning. It was going to be even crazier. It was never easy, but I never wanted to be with anyone except Bob.

CHAPTER 5

Summer and Siberia

IT WAS ALSO time now for us to make a living, and for me, to learn everything I could about farming. Bob was strong and had experience of working on the land, though not of running a business. I was starting from scratch. As I said, I had never seen a cow up close. I was way, way more of a city girl than a land girl.

In 1955, after arriving to live in south Wales, not only did I have an 'Alien card', but once a month I had a visit from a local policeman, who always arrived on his pushbike, just to make sure I was still here.

I was supposed to go to Pontypool Police Station to report but, as we had no car, it was decided to enlist the local bobby to see to the formalities.

That went on for quite a long time, and wherever I went I always had to have this alien card with me.

Moving to the Welsh valleys was something of a challenge. It wasn't hard to work out that I was different when I first arrived. People would say: 'You're not from this country, are you?' and I would tell them that I was from Holland. I suppose to some I might as well have said I'd just arrived from outer space.

The farm, back then, comprised 40 acres of land, much of which was woodland clinging to the steep hillside that overshadowed the farm.

We had a cowshed where we could tie up 15 milking cows, a mealhouse where the animal feed was kept, plus fertilizer which was spread every spring to encourage the grass to grow.

There was also a hay barn, two wooden sheds and a tractor. We used to borrow all machinery, like a roller, harrows, hay turner etc., from our well-to-do neighbour, Cecil Jenkins. (Oh yes, we did have a link box – a rectangular metal box for carrying animal food and equipment – to go behind the tractor.) Hedging was always done by hand, which was just about the most exhausting job on the farm, apart from haymaking. Nowadays every job on the farms is done by machines.

The woodland was and still is the place where our water supply comes from. When Bob first came here there was no water in the house, just a pump in the yard. All the mountains in Wales contain springs, so Bob decided to look for a water diviner to help him locate one of these springs near the top of the woodland.

This man used a very old and trusted method. He had two willow sticks which he held crossed in front of him while walking slowly up and down the woodland. When the sticks moved slightly downwards, it was a sign that water might be found in or near that spot. And it was!

So Bob set about building a water reservoir – the 'well' we called it – and used his horse and a cart to get his building materials up there. A gigantic job. The reservoir was built approximately 25 metres below the spring that the diviner had discovered.

Bob then piped the water from the spring to the reservoir and from there all the way down the fields into the house and the barn (cowshed). No pump was used as the whole thing was gravity-fed coming down the mountainside.

This remarkable system is still in use to this day and I hope will remain so for many more years to come. We always thought it was a small miracle. And all our own work! However, Bob never put any filters into the pipes and over the years this led to a few surprises. One morning, after a stormy night of rain, some tiny tadpoles plopped into the kitchen sink from the cold water tap! Another time, the water tasted a bit strange and was slightly discoloured, so we took a walk up to the 'well' and discovered to our horror that the livestock had moved its stone lid and there was a dead sheep inside! We duly removed the sheep, put the lid back in place, and boiled the water for a few days. We never seemed to get ill from any of this. I think we had nurtured a good immune system!

As mentioned already, Bob did have a man working on the farm called Tom Wheeler, but Bob paid him off when I arrived. The same thing happened with the horse, that too had to go when I arrived, but that was for another reason. I was totally petrified of the animal.

Jantien, my daughter, always believed that my fear of horses was connected to the prank on a Dutch farm when a boy put me on a horse and slapped it so that it galloped away out of control. I was nine at the time. She is probably correct.

Bob's horse used to roam freely around the yard and was young and frisky. I was getting used to cows, but that horse scared me.

There was also another man helping on the farm, called Glaswyn. He would come to help every now and then with potato planting and picking, mangold cutting and, of course, haymaking in the summer.

Summer time is the most wonderful season in the countryside. As the city girl in me subsided into memory, I liked all the seasons for different reasons. But the summers always had an extra magic.

Living itself is easier in the summer, being outside most of the day, so not so much time spent cooking. Fewer clothes are needed, less washing (no washing machine, anyway), the cows out grazing happily, not so much mucking out the cowshed.

On those blissful lighter evenings Bob and I never wanted to go in and sit down in the house. We used to sit on the steps outside the house with a cuppa, contemplating a new project like starting a vegetable plot, or trying our hand at being a bit more self-sufficient.

So, our first veggie plot was born, and there were more to follow on a different site. We sometimes used the services of Dai Mountain, an odd-jobber from Trevethin, who used to walk down the mountain looking for a spot of work here and there.

He was as strong as an ox and certainly knew how to dig. Within a few days he had dug over half of our plot, creating a large grassy area that in later life we called Wembley.

We did make mistakes, not all our gardening exploits turned out well. In the beginning we grew far too much, a common mistake we later found; 60 lettuces all ready at once was excessive!

The early winters in Wales were proper winters! Frost and snow usually started in December after a wet autumn, and some winters did not finish until halfway through April.

During the winter the cows would only be let out on the yard (in front of the house) so that the shed could be cleaned before letting them back in. They would stand around shivering in the freezing wind and would be pushing each other out of the way to go back into the warm shed.

But once spring arrived, the cows would be let out daily. On the first day out from their winter shed they would be a sight to see. They were so happy with their new-found freedom. They would jump around with their back legs kicking the air.

Before afternoon milking started, we would have 'tea', a big pot of tea with a variety of home-made cakes. By 5pm milking would start. In the meantime, I used to feed the calves with milk from a bucket. This milk was made from milk powder mixed with hot water, and then made up to the right consistency with cold water.

We always reared a few calves to replace the older cows, and of course without calves there is no milk! Our bull calves went to market within a week, which at the beginning I found heartbreaking, especially when hearing the mothers bellowing for days on end, standing by the gate with their painfully swollen udders.

But that was usually just for a few days. Then they would forget all about their little calves. We never had a bull and used artificial insemination on our cows, which was cheaper but not always that reliable. Nowadays farmers seem to keep bulls again. The winters here felt cold. The draught would literally whistle through the house because of ill-fitting windows, and the fact that most houses in Wales at that time did not have any insulation, either in the walls or the roof space.

Old Welsh cottages used to have enormous fireplaces; so big that people could actually sit right inside them, on benches called 'settles' to keep warm. The fireplace in Persondy was also built that way, but most of the back was filled in some years ago, and the fire basket was brought forward so that the room could be a little warmer. This work was done by Bob and two friends in 1963, whilst I had taken the two little ones to Holland for a short break.

The Rayburn, although dusty and needing regular refuelling and de-ashing, was a godsend. At least the kitchen was warm.

The waste pipes in the bathroom regularly froze, because this room was built facing north, and these pipes would be on the outside of the house instead of being built on the inside of the wall, as they are today. So, when this happened, we would wash ourselves in the kitchen sink.

The cattle would be indoors in the barn throughout the winter, but there was a time when we had a few too many young heifers as replacements for some of the other 'ladies'. The mealhouse was full of cow and chicken food and fertiliser sacks for the spring, so there were no other buildings where these heifers could be housed – they had to stay out in the field.

One Christmas day, when the snow was very deep, we sat down to our turkey dinner in very festive mood when, just outside the kitchen window, there appeared our heifers. They were bellocking loudly and nuzzling the window panes. It was such a pitiful sight.

Bob had put hay out earlier, but there was another reason for their dismay – the 'bosh' (water source) outside was empty, so they could not drink, and the inlet pipes were frozen. There was nothing else for it but to get the long hose from outside and fill the bosh from the tap over the kitchen sink. The long hose was draped along the kitchen table (on which our Christmas dinner was ready to eat) and then out of the kitchen window straight into the bosh (which is still there to this day). That was a very chilly Christmas dinner!

Bob had at least taught me how to lay the fire in the living room when the first chill of winter arrived. I was used to central heating in my parents' house in Amsterdam. We were far more advanced over there with the heating of houses, even during the late 1940s. Persondy was a long way behind!

The open fire in the living room was only lit in the evening, because we would not be sitting down until the evening's milking was finished.

At around 10 o'clock at night we would go and lay hay for the cows and just check everything, then douse the fire and go to bed. I kept socks and jumpers on to keep me from freezing. No wonder our son Alan used, in later years, to refer to the place as being Siberia.

*

My first year of marriage to Bob was spent mainly trying to make the house a home and also getting used to befriending the cows, chickens, and one pig (a sow) with a litter of eight piglets. I have to say there is nothing in the world so gorgeous as a newborn piglet! They feel soft as velvet with their silky downy skin, and they are toasty warm. Unfortunately, they do grow up!

There was also a sheepdog who was quite friendly but was never allowed in the house. He always slept in the hay barn. A sheepdog is supposed to help with moving sheep (in our case, cows) from A to B, but our dog never seemed to get that message. I do remember him once valiantly herding all the neighbouring farmer's cows into my flower garden, just as I was trying to chase them out!

The Rayburn stove was used to cook on and supply hot water for the day. We burned coal and wood in it. I used to get up just after Bob to see to this thing and have it roaring to cook on and the water good and hot for cleaning down after milking.

After breakfast the stove would be turned down for the rest of the morning until preparations for dinner would be made at 12 o'clock. Yes, midday, but that was the norm with all the farming people around here.

Dinner would be fairly similar every day – meat and two veg. Bob grew potatoes and, in the winter, we always had some vegetables like kale and turnips, which were grown for cow fodder over here. Not in Holland though; these were all sold in shops for human consumption.

Of course, I bought things like peas, beans and onions etc. in town. There was always a pudding, usually a tart. I cannot imagine how we ever did any work after all that food. Bob then used to have a quick forty winks, feet up on the mantelpiece. I would wash up. Bob would go back to work outside.

We also had a few hundred chickens, and had a contract with British Nylon Spinners, a large new factory just down the road, to deliver 30 chickens, ready dressed, to their main canteen twice a month, every other Saturday.

In those days the heads and feet of these chickens had to be scrubbed with hot water and left in place, with the heart and liver pushed through the wings. What a job! I was later told that this was so, so that people could see what kind of birds they were, whether a hen or a cockerel.

Bob killed the birds and plucked them. I dressed and weighed. I remember Bob coming into the kitchen with the first two birds, killed and plucked and still very warm, and then proceeding to show me how to do the cleaning and dressing.

The worktop we used in the kitchen was made of an old door, sitting on a bit of a cupboard which Bob had made for me when I first came. l used it for many years.

When I was ready to attack this poor chicken, I put my hand up its backside to draw out all the innards. Suddenly there came a long drawn-out squawk, which sent me screaming to the other end of the kitchen!

It was the air inside which had been pushed through the wind pipe of the chicken as I put my hand inside. Bob had a good laugh but it was a very long time till I felt like joining him back on chicken duty.

But then I managed to get into the swing of things, which was just as well as we had to do all this work, plus milking in between, in one day. Then we delivered the next day so that all these birds would be fresh.

Every day at 4 o'clock Bob would get the cows in, helped (or hindered) by our lovely sheepdog Titch. We never had a dog or a cat at home in Amsterdam, so the fact that this dog was not allowed indoors was fine with me, as I tried my very best to keep the place reasonably clean.

At least I tried. People visiting always kept their wellies on coming into the house, even if they had waded through the cow muck – which took a lot of getting used to. I did make a sign once on a piece of cardboard, respectfully asking visitors to take off their wellies by the front door. It was a token effort. Can you imagine the laughter from visiting Welsh farmers?

As there was very little money to spend on things for the house, I put our wedding present, the sewing machine, to good use at last. After I had made the bedroom and bathroom curtains out of my wedding dress, I made curtains for the rest of the house from some material I bought at Pontypool market. The result was quite pleasing and our house was starting to look more like a home.

Haymaking was the most important job of the year. We had to try and make sure there was enough fodder for the winter months. The weather was somewhat more reliable in those days, so one could more or less count on fair weather during June and July, apart from an occasional shower.

A few fields would be shut off from when the grass grows its best, at the beginning of May, and usually by the second week in June mowing would start.

In our case the trouble was that, as we had no machinery (apart from a tractor and link box), we had to wait until Cecil Jenkins, our neighbouring farmer, had mown his own fields first so we could borrow his mower.

Once the grass was mown it had to dry, be turned, and turned again and finally raked into neat lines with the turner, which we also had to borrow. Bob and I raked a lot of it by hand with pitchforks, before the dried-out grass could be baled.

If the weather was set fair a field could be ready to be baled within a few days, but if rain was threatening you can imagine the stress in the air when waiting for the turner or the baling machine to turn up, which was always operated by Cecil.

Once the hay was baled most of the farmers would help each other. Local lads would also come and help after work to get all the bales in before nightfall. By the end of July our Dutch barn would be full to the top. It was very, very hard work, even though I was gradually getting accustomed to the manual labour. Aching backs and blistered hands come to mind, but there was also something special about that time, the feeling of satisfaction that you get when the big job is done and also the camaraderie amongst the men … and me.

In between helping I would get food and drink from the house, and we would have a short break. The food would usually be cake, home-made elderflower pop, ginger beer and a flask of tea.

In the evening, after the hauling and before the pub closing time, the menfolk would go to the Star. Bob and I never went to the pub in those days. Ladies did not go there, anyway. I cannot imagine that now.

I still hear everybody joking and laughing in the semi-darkness, bringing in the last load or two on wobbly trailers full of bales. How different farming is today. Everything is done with huge machines by two people, with no physical work and all you hear is industrial noise!

There were two events in the year that I looked forward

to enormously. In the early years of our marriage we would be invited to the Christmas 'hunt ball' with Bob's horsey family, and later there was the Harvest Supper dance in Little Mill village hall. I would spend weeks looking forward to it, altering a dress to wear and anticipating the music and dancing. I would have butterflies of excitement, but Bob hated going out and invariably he would come down with a last-minute cold or upset tummy. Strangely, he was always fine the following morning! But we did go to a few Harvest Supper dances over the years. These were to celebrate the end of harvest every autumn when 'everything was safely gathered in'. They were lovely evenings with all the local farmers and their families, waltzing the night away!

I have always loved to dance, and any chance to go to or host a party was always wonderful. As we got older, Bob would enjoy New Year's Eve parties which we hosted with lots of home-made wine. He was never keen to go out anywhere else!

I learned how to make home-made wine in my forties and threw myself into it.

Wine was expensive then, and to have plenty for very little money was attractive! I would make gallons of it with windfall apples, pears, plums, damsons and anything else available! There were always many buckets of fermenting juice bubbling away in the hallway, promising all sorts of delights for the following year. Many a visitor went home extremely happy after an evening with us on the apple wine.

*

The little setbacks and the Christmas Day trauma with the thirsty cows made us realize that we could no longer keep that number of cows on our small acreage. So we sold a few of the older cows. That meant, of course, that our income went down and then the price of milk also took a dip.

One day, a letter arrived from our bank manager requesting a meeting with us as soon as possible. This was always a very scary situation, as we knew we had no money. Tidy clothes were ironed and shoes cleaned.

We arrived and sat down, and he sat there looking a little grim. The outcome was that our overdraft facilities had expired, and the £2,000 debt, a very large sum in those days, had to be repaid.

It was a huge blow and we were devastated. But neither of us believed in feeling sorry for ourselves. There was only one way out. It was an awful decision to have to make but Bob decided the best way out was to sell our land, all of it. It was sold privately, and obviously the two interested parties were the two farmers either side of us, Joe Williams and Jim Goldsmith. It wasn't a contest really; Joe owned one of the biggest farms around.

With the money we paid off all our debts. The cows and tractor were sold off as well of course, so the place became eerily quiet. We still had chickens in battery cages, a line of work that was not very successful. The overdraft was paid off, but our lovely farmland was gone.

Now, what should we do with what was left of the farm? We lived for a while without any income, except for family allowance. Bob did a lot of repair work around the place and renewed a few gates. But what was the next stage? We had to earn.

Then one afternoon we had a visit from a representative of a company called Thornborrows. He told us about a new way of chicken farming. He sounded very interesting. So after another meeting we decided to go for this type of chicken keeping.

Thornborrows operated a major breeding operation for chicks. They sent them out to various locations to be raised – more freedom for the chickens and therefore better egg production. That was the theory.

So we built a deep litter house where the chickens could run free on deep straw.

We got rid of the old battery cages we had, sold the chickens we kept before, and used that chicken house also to start this new chicken farm. Bob built long rows of nest boxes, and perches where the chickens could roost at night.

Thornborrows provided us with 1,000 day-old chicks. We then sold the resulting eggs to them on a contract basis. The chicks arrived one day all packed in cardboard boxes, including cockerel chicks of course. It was 25 chicks to one cockerel.

But we needed more space. Luckily Thornborrows also provided a small wooden shed which arrived just before the chicks. To our horror, we found that it was a sort of flat-pack, and was not completely built and ready. We got some help from Mr Routledge, a big burly Yorkshireman, to erect the shed more professionally. But, in the meantime, these 1,000 chicks had to spend the first few days in our hallway! Utter chaos was just not the word for the scene, or the mess. Or the smell!

The chicks were out of their boxes and under a two-metre long 'brooder', which provided warmth and light.

The hallway in those days was very basic, like the rest of the house, with a concrete floor and a few pieces of furniture, a grandfather clock and a chest.

The cheeping at times was ear-piercing, and it was my job to look after them with food and water, and check that they were healthy. Actually, it was a job that I loved though. In farming terms it was a world away from the cows.

After a few days the shed, or hut as we called it, was ready and we transported the lot from the hallway to their new home. The hallway was left covered with a fine white dust which went everywhere, including up your nose, and took many days to get rid of.

When they were approximately six weeks old, we transferred the chicks to 'lay boxes' in the field to harden them up. They had wire runs and slept inside at night. We had a long row of these boxes all along one field. This was just before the last of our land was sold off.

After some time they were moved to the big sheds, which were by then ready and waiting. Somewhat shakily, we had started a new business.

The chickens, as they were now, had to learn how to roost at dusk. Bob and I would go inside the sheds and pick all the youngsters up, sometimes three at the time and put them on the perches. If that was not done at this particular time, the birds would pile on top of one another to go to sleep and consequently be smothered.

We did lose a few that way, but the procedure would carry on every evening for a week or two until the birds had learned to perch. And roost.

Once the birds started laying, the eggs piled up and we spent a large part of the day collecting eggs by the bucketful. These eggs were not for commercial use but for breeding, so they had to be kept in a warm place.

So they stayed in our kitchen, in wooden boxes holding large trays which were to be collected once a week. The next hurdle was that the Thornborrows' lorries were huge, and so they struggled to come up our drive.

No dirty eggs were accepted, so we had to wash them in the kitchen sink – hundreds of them – but not soak them, which would have affected fertility. We were paid a price per dozen and a bonus on top for the percentage of fertility.

All the chickens were replaced once a year, and the sheds cleaned out (a back-breaking job, all done by hand). By the time the next huge batch of tiny chicks arrived, we finally started to earn some money. We did the whole cycle again, rearing, roosting, delivering, clearing up, and maintained it for another year or two after that.

Then the price of eggs dropped, and the type of deep litter house we used to house our chickens was not good enough any more due to new regulations. We were offered a new contract but, reading through the pages, it became obvious that we could not carry on with keeping chickens the way we did.

New requirements were, for instance, windowless houses with electric lights staying on day and night. There needed to be much larger premises and a new minimum of 3,000 chicks to start with. Imagine having 3,000 chirping chicks!

To carry on we needed to repair our chicken houses, add more every year, and that may well have put us back into debt again. Bob was determined to carry on farming in some way, so we had hard thinking to do. But the chicks project was now out of the question. Subsistence farming was tough! But it taught us to use our initiative.

Next up? 'Intensive farming' I believe is what it was called at the time, and this time it was with pigs. The old cowshed was used for hoarding all manner of things, so we decided to clear it out and clean it completely. Enter the pigs.

Some time went by, possibly a year, where we just lived on the bit of money we had left in the bank, plus the family allowance. So whilst the pig planning was still on hold, Bob had to find some other work. We just did not have enough money.

Our neighbour, Cecil Jenkins, offered Bob a job as cowman, looking after 120 milking cows. He stayed there for nearly two years. His wages were £17 per week; there was no overtime pay, although Bob often stayed late into the evening, especially if a cow was calving. The work was very hard, but at least it was an income.

In the meantime, we had started to buy a few pigs (one at the time). Bob had built pig pens in the empty barn and we quietly started to fill them.

While Bob was at Cecil's farm, I looked after the pigs. We started with five sows, which we bought 'in pig', that is, pregnant. Little piglets started to be born, and the feeling was good. We were back in farming again, and we never minded hard work.

Bob's brother Seymour would come with his family once a year. The highlight for me was when he would open the boot of his car to display a huge array of Yardley's cosmetics samples. I could rummage to my heart's content, choosing lipsticks, foundation, eyeshadows – everything a girl could want. One rule, throughout my life, has been to always put my make-up on and arrange my hair nicely at the start of the day, never mind the task ahead! A girl should always look her best! Yardley's also came in handy on the farm, helping our self-sufficient, no-money lifestyle. Young pigs have to be injected with antibiotics at a young age in order to stay healthy. But rounding up the squealing creatures, and keeping track of which ones you had injected, was no mean feat. The pigs needed marking, and Yardley's 'Vintage Rose' lipstick worked a treat! I remember one year one of my nieces from Holland came to stay for the summer and she helped out on the farm. Her face was a picture of open-mouthed astonishment when she saw me using expensive lipstick to mark big Xs on the piglets!

However, the breeding side of the business was to strike unlucky. We bought a boar as an investment but it became lame. In the end his back legs would collapse every time he tried to stand up, so that was the end of him. A boar that can't mount a sow is no use!

So, more thinking. We then decided to change from breeding to fattening pigs, and signed a contract with a company called FMC, who would supply us with 50 weaners (eight-week-old pigs) and we would fatten these to a certain weight. After a period of roughly six months, FMC would buy them back from us.

Again, they had a huge lorry. So for our delivery they sent a special smaller one and things started to take off. In the beginning we fed the sows and their litters, and later the weaners, on meal, which was delivered once a month by Newcombe, and later by Pauls. This proved to be very expensive food. Prices went up and up, and we thought that our pig ambitions would go the way of the cows and chicks. I still loved my life with Bob, but the farming life had become a struggle again.

With no fields, only our buildings to use, our subsistence farm needed constant change and new ideas in order to survive. We were so tired every evening but we still laughed together as we dragged our weary selves up the winding stairs to bed each night. One day we saw an advert in the local paper, inviting tenders for the collection of waste from schools and hospitals. This waste was left-over food.

Here was a chance, again, to maybe make our business a bit more profitable and avoid the expensive feedstuffs. We were successful with our tender and were allocated an area starting from Pontypool and Penygarn to Trevethin, then to Cwmbran and Croesyceiliog, and on to Newport and Caerleon, Llanfrechfa and Ponthir, Raglan, Usk, New Inn and Abergavenny.

Again, it was a major task. We bought a van and a few dustbins (the old-fashioned metal type), but ended up getting quite a few second-hand plastic ones, 18 in all, which filled the van. It was a dirty, messy, back-breaking job, lifting bins heavy with left-over dinners into a van. Eighteen times per trip, two or three trips a day, to feed pigs that seemed to have bottomless stomachs!

Again, fate had played a trick. By the time we had made a start collecting all the food waste (mountains of it!), we had a letter from the council saying that all waste food collected now had to be 'steamed' (though it was all cooked already) as an extra precaution against foot and mouth disease.

A steamer. Where can you find a steamer? Quickly. Through a 'free-ads' newspaper we found one for sale in

Pontypool, in a laundrette business. An enormous thing. We had it removed and brought out to us on the back of a lorry. This was followed by a crane to lift the thing off again and install it in part of the mealhouse. More money needed – again!

Bob and I looked at the steamer in disbelief and spent ages working out the instructions. We had to stoke the boiler with coal and any old rubbish for an hour or so to get the correct pressure, so that steam would escape through little holes in piping inside the bottom of a big tank full of swill. It would rattle and clank and emit huge clouds of steam like some monster!

The pressure would have to remain high for at least half an hour to sterilise the food. It then had to cool down before the pigs could be fed. You would think that all this work and expense would have put us off, but it was our last bash at farming and we were not going to give up.

And at the end of the day we had to wash all the bins, and the rooms they were kept in, in preparation for the same rigmarole the following day. It was dirty and heavy work but we were never afraid of that, and we carried on for many years with the waste, the steamer and the pigs. We made some money at last.

We kept moving forwards. Once the dinner ladies at some of the schools from which we collected food found out that we had pigs, they wanted to know if we sold pork for the deep freeze. Most people had chest freezers in those days, which could easily hold half to a whole pig, all cut up in proper joints. Of course we obliged, and started a little sideline of selling deep freeze pork.

Our good friend Ed Lewis showed me how to joint a pig and lent me a few tools to start. We scrubbed out the mealhouse and took two pigs to the slaughterhouse in Abergavenny. That was the start. The sideline really took off and soon we spent most weekends cutting up and delivering, as friends and neighbours spread the word.

Well, it was not long before this little venture was stopped as well. We did feel a little cursed. The Ministry of Health declared suddenly that only butchers were to sell pork for the deep freeze, unless you could prove that your premises were tiled from top to bottom and had hot and cold running water.

Also, some nasty person reported us to the tax office in Pontypool. We were always paid in cash for all that deep freeze meat, you see. We were asked to visit the inspector there. Our accountant came as well, and he was worried in case we had not declared any extra income.

But we knew we were clear, because every penny had to go in the bank and we never made enough to pay any tax. We never went on that Caribbean cruise, though! In fact, we never went anywhere. The very idea never appealed to Bob.

The meeting with the tax inspector ended well, with a jolly and laughing atmosphere. We never found out who told on us. But I do have a good idea!

CHAPTER 6

The Boy and the Beetroot

ALAN WAS BORN right in the middle of a heat wave in June 1957 and, suddenly, we two were three. I had looked forward to this event tremendously. I was very lucky, and went through pregnancy without a hitch. I was slightly sick in the morning, with an aversion to, of all things, pickles.

Apart from that, everything carried on as normal. I helped Bob outside as much as possible, but managed to add the odd half-hour rest after lunch, or rather dinner as the midday meal was always called in those days.

I had no idea what the birth would entail. I didn't have any books about the subject. There were no classes, and as we didn't have a car at that time I never went any further than Pontypool – where there were no bookshops.

Anyway, none of that bothered me. I just told myself that I had seen a cow calving, so it must all be similar. There was no one to ask, you see. Well, there was Bob's family, but we never saw them, and anyway one did not talk about these sorts of things. It was all so different from today. Even at home in Holland, the birth of a baby was never discussed.

The only female amongst the farmers that used to call was Marge Lewis, who lived with her husband at Marge's parents' farm which was called Green Meadow, three or four fields away. I saw her very occasionally and it turned out that she was pregnant about the same time too.

Alan was born in June and David, her first born, arrived in the previous March. I did walk over a few times when we were both pregnant, but the amazing thing was that we never really talked about our condition. Of course, she had her mother, so that helped her.

The day came when I noticed a little discharge, and from my couple of visits to our doctor I thought things had finally started. (I was then two weeks overdue.)

Bob phoned Cecil Jenkins, our farming neighbour, who came round with his wife Kath, and the four of us drove to Cefn Ila, a country house just outside Usk which at the time was a maternity unit. You had the choice; you could go there for the birth, or Pontypool Hospital. Cefn Ila was close by and small, with just a handful of staff, no doctor, just a matron.

A doctor could be summoned if things did not go as normal, which happened in my case. I started having contractions on the Friday morning, and Al was not born until the Saturday evening at 7pm.

It was a forceps job in the end. He was a big baby, for my slender loins. He weighed 8 pounds 7 ounces, was perfectly formed, had slightly tanned skin, and big eyes which were wide open as soon as he was born. The only noise he made was a polite sneeze.

In those days nearly everybody smoked, and so when I was wheeled back to my bed in the ward I was so jubilant and so, so happy. There were another three beds in that ward and I threw everyone else a cigarette. We all lit up and enjoyed the rest of that evening. One just cannot imagine that today; then you were just allowed to smoke whenever you felt like it.

The nurses had telephoned Bob and found him halfway through milking. So he had to finish that first. He then came out to see us, Al in the nursery downstairs and I upstairs.

Bob came in looking very suntanned, and wearing a shirt with both sleeves missing. Apparently, our sow had got out the day before and bashed down the pole which held up the washing line. Luckily, there was not much washing on it, except one of Bob's shirts, which was well chewed by the animal. One sleeve was ruined, so Bob decided to rip the other sleeve off as well. As you do.

The nurses were all mad about Bob. They thought he was such a handsome man with his black hair and bright blue eyes and tanned face. I was proud of my two handsome boys, and tried to forget about the shirt.

In those days you had to rest for two weeks after the confinement. You could walk around outside in the beautiful gardens that belonged to this house in one's dressing gown, but every afternoon we had to go to bed for a good two hours' sleep or rest.

Three meals a day, good food, all cooked to get our strength back, or so we were told. Visiting was only allowed in the evening. But despite the rest and the relative luxury, I was very homesick after a few days. I missed Bob and the farm, especially during that beautiful summer weather. I just wanted to go home with my new little bundle. I felt totally fit and also very bored.

But rules were rules and, looking back, it was a damned good job that this rest period was enforced. That is another aspect definitely very different today. I spent most of my time there writing to my mother and the rest of my family. Bob sent a telegram to my parents, but that was the only contact in those days. Phoning home was simply not an option in 1957, at least not for us. Writing letters was what everybody did.

Every morning Matron would come around the wards with a handful of mail. She always knew which letters were mine without looking at the name, because my letters were the only ones written on airmail paper and envelopes. How I used to look forward to them.

The day came when I was allowed home. Bob had managed to get a second-hand pick-up truck whilst I was in Cefn Ila. It was a beautiful blue-sky morning and I was so excited that my blood pressure – which was always taken before being allowed home – had suddenly jumped up. This was in the morning, so I was told to sit on the bed and rest for a couple of hours.

Eventually my blood pressure returned to almost normal and one of the nurses telephoned Bob to tell him he could come to fetch me. I had asked Bob to bring me a dress, sandals and the other usual bits and pieces, like underwear plus a set of nappies (one thick, one thin and a pair of plastic pants) and of course something for our little Al to wear (babygrows were not around in those days). I had put all these things ready in a bag before I went in.

The dress was very pretty, but one could not say it fitted well. My poor bosoms was totally squashed and poured over the top of the fairly low neckline, and the zip on the side of the dress was a total no-no. Anyway, off we went home.

When we reached home I put Al on the settee in our living room with a small blanket around him whilst I went upstairs to find something else to wear. A loud shout from Bob downstairs made me run down. The cows had got out and were roaming all around the yard and the drive. There was nothing else for it but to get out there to help.

Little Al was fast asleep. Good job, with all this commotion going on. My milk glands were doing overtime, and I was soon a dripping mess down the front of my shirt. We finally managed to get the cows in the cowshed – it was nearly milking time anyway – and went back in the house to admire our new baby son who had not moved an inch, but was still sleeping peacefully.

At five years old he went to school in New Inn. I used to walk with him in the morning to catch the school bus at the Star pub. I would wait for him there at 4.15 every afternoon when he returned. In those days the first-year children were allowed to have a little rest in the afternoon, on little benches if needed. This was a very good idea for the country children, who would be away from home all day. Town children were allowed to go home at midday for an hour for lunch. Al and other country children had a cooked lunch in school.

*

Jantien was born in February 1959; not in a heat wave! It was a freezing cold night with deep snow. My mother had decided to come over for the birth of this little babe. Apparently, she was quite upset when she was not invited to be here for Alan's birth. I didn't realise that, but she told me later.

She arrived by boat and bus all the way from Amsterdam, a week in advance in case the baby decided to come early. I had spring cleaned the house, done the washing (no machine of course, just a boiler and a wringer) and also painted two doors of a cupboard on which the aluminium sink stood. I found a tin of cheerful red paint, and transformed (so I thought) the look of the scruffy cupboard.

Before my mother came I had sewn myself a new nightie for the confinement. Bob and I never wore night clothes and I wore it the night before my mother arrived. Before getting into bed I wanted to get myself a glass of water. There was no glass in the bathroom so I went downstairs to get one from the kitchen. I switched on the tap and realized there was something holding me back.

My brand-new nightie was stuck against the wet red paint, right over my bump. I had forgotten all about it! The language was not pretty and Bob came running downstairs wondering what had happened. He helped me off with the nightie, which went straight in the bin.

Bob and I went to fetch my mother the next day from Newport bus station. She had had to change in Cheltenham on the way from London, poor thing, so she had had a very long drawn-out journey, especially as the M4 had not yet been built then.

This time I had the baby at home. I had that choice, although our doctor, Dr Michael, was none too happy about my choice. He told me he would attend the birth if possible. The midwife would be in control of everything.

My mother started to lay down the law. She went into our bedroom, which was separated from the landing by a plasterboard wall running from the stairs to the airing cupboard. She looked at our bed and immediately ordered Bob into the spare room. She and Bob brought one of the spare beds into our bedroom next to our big bed on which she slept – all to give me undisturbed sleep and plenty of room.

Bob was not very happy at that decision. Neither was I, but it was not time to rock any boats and we did what she suggested. Alan slept in the spare room as well. He was one and a half years old by then.

There was no heating of any kind upstairs of course. So we put a little electric fire on the windowsill in our bedroom, for when the birth happened. A few days went by, in which I tried to show my mother how to cook on the Rayburn, which was all so different for her. Bob would see to the fuel for that stove and also light the open fire in the living room before milking. So, my mother did not freeze to death – she was used, of course, to a fabulous, centrally-heated house in Amsterdam.

The first week of her stay went by and nothing happened on the birth front. My father actually telephoned (a big event in those days) to find out what was going on, but no baby had appeared.

The driving force of running the household in Amsterdam was missing, and according to my father, who loved his routine, things were getting out of hand.

On the Friday night things started moving at last. I could feel the first contractions starting and, not wanting to wake my mother who was fast asleep next to my bed, I buried my head under the blankets and held my breath until the contractions faded.

My mother was too vigilant, and she heard me after all. She switched on the light and sat next to me on the bed, huddled in a blanket. Bob and Alan in the bedroom next door were peacefully asleep, so we whispered about things for a time, my mother refusing to go back to sleep.

The morning came and with it much stronger contractions. So it was decided to call the midwife, Nurse Wilks from Goetre. Another potential area of concern. During the night there had been a very heavy fall of snow and the road to our house was difficult in such weather.

Bob had the inspired idea of employing the tractor, with the link box on the back, to get Nurse Wilks, the thinking being that Nurse Wilks would sit in the link box. She had different ideas, and decided to come in her car and risk it. As the snow was still very fresh, she thought she could just about make it.

No phone call was made. So, as Bob was sliding down the drive with brakes on, he met Nurse Wilks coming in the other direction, They collided head on, and she just managed to get to the end of the drive. No way to welcome the midwife! There was an impact, but not too much damage was done to her car, and we had to clear up the formalities later.

Nurse Wilks was a lovely old lady, due for retirement. She was 65, small, plump and very cheerful, with a wicked sense of humour. My poor mother could not understand her Welsh accent at all, so those two used a lot of sign language, which was very funny. Also, my mother was a tall lady, so they looked such a comical duo.

Bob was snowed under, almost literally, with work outside. We had chicks (at a stage before they were fully grown) in hayboxes in one of our fields. Of course, these were covered in snow so had to be sorted out. The adult chickens, the laying hens, were all in the big houses in the yard, so they were all right.

Egg collecting was more difficult. We collected three times a day in large buckets, and with snow thick on the ground all these tasks became a bit more difficult.

By five in the afternoon the next day, Dr Michael turned up to check on the progress of the birth. After a quick examination he told me that the last stage of the birth would not be long, and left. Two hours later Jantien was born, a screaming little beetroot, weighing in at 7 pounds and 8 ounces.

My mother immediately held her in a towel in front of the electric fire, as the air was still so cold for our little babe. Nurse Wilks opened the landing window and shouted for Bob to come up to see his little daughter. Men were never present at the birth in those days, not that Bob ever wanted to be.

It was a while until I heard him on the stairs. He peered his head, with the flat cap he always wore, around the bedroom door. His face broke into a huge smile as he came closer to see this little bundle, now quiet.

He looked at her in amazement for some time. He admitted that he had been hoping for a little girl, so happiness was universal. When the question of a name came up, we had a bit of a shock. If the baby was a little girl we wanted to call her Helen (the name of my dear daughter-in-law later in life).

My mother flatly refused. She made quite a thing about

it. She said that name was not right as it sounded too much like Alan. In Holland we pronounce Alan as Ellen, so there was a problem.

Thinking caps on again for another name. Two days went by without any decision.

In the end we called her Jantien, after my grandmother in Holland whom she never saw as she died two months later. It was my mother's idea, and Bob and I were both happy.

I was up the next day to resume my role downstairs and outside, again to the annoyance of the nurse who had told me to stay in bed for at least a week, as was the norm in those days. But I felt good enough to go downstairs and little Al kept wanting his mam. He was not allowed to go upstairs, as I was supposed to rest.

My mother left for Holland a few days later, having really bonded with Jant (as we call her now). She was worn out, poor thing, trying so hard to fit in with our strange and difficult way of living, so, so different from the city life she was used to. Bless her.

Bob and I loved her to bits and really missed her when she was gone. Country life she may have loved eventually, but the farming, no.

Jant grew up into a busy bubbly little girl and her first school day came along on 1 September 1964.

She met the school bus at the Star pub at 8am, came back at four in the afternoon, just like her brother. She absolutely loved her first day and chatted non-stop according to Miss Waters, the teacher in the reception class at New Inn Infant School.

Bob and I had successfully launched two young lives.

CHAPTER 7

On the Buses

WE HAD DONE our best to make a living out of farming with the various changes we had made. After the arrival of the two children we were still seeking our fortune or, at least, something consistent. With two young children we needed to think about profit, not just our preferred and happy farming existence.

Out of the blue I was offered a job as the driver of a school minibus. I decided to take the plunge. Our good friend George Vater had a fleet of buses servicing many local schools, and was always looking for more drivers. The driving job was ideal for me, and would bring in a little more money for the pot.

To start with I had to sit another driving exam, because the bus I was to drive would be a Passenger Service Vehicle. I got a badge which you wore every time you went out to pick up passengers – in this case school children between the ages of four and 18. The Vaters helped me learn the theory and pass the test. I enjoyed the work.

After a year driving for George, he suggested that I bought one of his buses, as he replaced one each year. We decided on a fair price, which my darling brother Herman wanted to lend to us. We could pay him back in stages, which we did within the year... well almost!

This meant that I could start up my own business, which would come under the name of R&H Francis. I now had to apply for another licence to do this work, and after a while I had a letter requesting me to attend an appointment at Transport House in Cardiff, where I had to 'put my case'.

We were amazed at the amount of people there, all applying or re-applying for a PSV operators' licence. Some of the firms there I recognised, such as Capitol, Trumans and others. All had brought a solicitor along with them to speak on their behalf.

The whole spectacle looked like a court room, with everyone standing up as the Traffic Commissioner took his seat. In Holland we would have called it a *poppenkast* [puppet show].

Some licences were granted, some were refused, and I came up right at the end. I had to walk to the front, step onto a stand, give my name and address and explain why I wanted this licence (as it was my first one as an operator). It was a world away from keeping pigs!

Well, I did my best and added that I would very soon own two buses. I thought that might help, and it did. I was granted a licence to operate two buses, and not only did I get a national licence but also an international licence, which of course I never did make use of and never even asked for.

George had come with me and he sat at the back of the room. He was stunned. He was never given an international licence and he had been in the game for years.

Our premises had to conform – there had to be a garage where the buses would be parked at night, and it had to be generally tidy. Guess what. Bob had already built the garage, and we passed all the requirements.

Our first bus was a Commer, and I was very proud of it. We then needed to win a 'contract'. In order to do that, you had to 'tender' a price that was the lowest bid for a particular school run. It was always a really difficult decision – what price should we tender? Too little and we wouldn't make any money, AGAIN, but too much and we wouldn't win the contract. George Vater was a good friend and helped us. We won a contract for 12 pick-ups locally. The contracts lasted for one year only in those days, but after a few years that was changed to three years, so much better. There was a lot of competition, especially as a lot of people were made redundant at that time from places like the ICI company here in Mamheilad. Some of these people would use their redundancy money to buy a minibus and apply for contracts.

George was a really good help to me, showing me the pitfalls when applying or re-applying for new contracts. He said we should never try to take contracts away from others because they would get us next time.

We used to get tender forms for contracts just before Christmas. There was a long list of them, so you could take your pick of areas you were interested in. Over Christmas we would be hoping and praying that we would get at least some of the contracts we had applied for. The post at the beginning of January would bring us the answers – it was a very tense time!

We bought our second bus from George, a black Bedford, and sold the Commer. Our new contracts took us much further afield, with pick-ups to and from Tintern and St Arvans, to Hafodyrynys. This was transport for mentally and physically handicapped children, needing two escorts to look after them.

Things moved on. We sold the black Bedford and slowly acquired two more Bedfords from George and increased our contracts accordingly. Could I persuade Bob to join the business? He was not keen; he said that farming was his job, but as the pig business was never going to make much money, it was a great fill-in.

So Bob also took his PSV driving test and came into my little business. Once a year I took the buses to be inspected at New Inn. I was the only woman around in that type of work; that has all changed now.

We were also lucky with community connections. John Jones, who owned a garage in Goetre, provided our petrol and repair station. He looked after our buses well, so they would pass the inspection every year. Jon and Grace Jones became good friends over the years.

Unlike some of our farming exploits, our bus contracts got better and better. At times we were awarded more than we could handle, so we had to buy another bus from George. This time another Bedford, so we now had three.

And our local contacts, typical of a Welsh community I suppose, again helped us. Jones from the garage had a daughter-in-law, and I took her for a test drive to check her suitability. She sat her PSV exam, passed first time, and joined us on the road.

We got on very well, and she was happy with her wages, thoroughly reliable and good at her job. There was no margin for error; you had to be safe of course and also to be a good time-keeper to get everyone to school on time. It was a pity that some of the parents did not understand that.

Then came a time when there were contracts coming out for taxis as well. These contracts, as long as one had a Hackney licence, could also be used for school children. We were on a roll. We bought an Austin 1800, quite old, but in good condition and working order.

There was one long seat in the back, which could seat three school children, plus the front passenger seat. These cars made ideal taxis; they were roomy and very sturdy.

Local knowledge again. Ann, a sister of Dai the mountain, had a fully comp licence, so we didn't even have to advertise for a driver. She was great at the job and she could keep the car at home when not in use, a lot easier all round.

Then one day we had a phone call from my brother Herman. He was ringing from London, where he and his family had been living for a year or two. He had moved there from Singapore.

Herman and his wife Paddy and the two sons were planning to come to Mamheilad for the weekend, which they did quite often. The plan was to come by car and return to London by train – leaving their car here, as they wanted us to have it. Herman was being moved by the bank yet again, back to Canada, to the headquarters of the Bank of Montreal where he was later made a director.

It was a second-hand car, which they really did not use much in London and they simply did not want the hassle of selling it. So leaving it here for us was the best solution – not least for us. All the bad luck and roadblocks we had come across as farmers seemed to be replaced by good news.

This car was not as big as the 1800 but there was enough room for two children in the back and the third in

By 1880, in an effort to stop an exodus of the wealthy to Haarlem (overcrowding and sanitation in the central canal areas was a problem) beautiful new houses were developed around the city's parks. Hanny grew up in Oranje Nassaulaan 13, very close to the Vondelpark.

Hanny's parents – the professor (Herman Dooyeweerd) and Jantiena. Unusually, he looks like he is breaking into a smile.

The five eldest siblings, outside No. 13, probably around 1937. Hanny is the youngest, and is bottom left.

Aeneas Mackay School, Amsterdam. Hanny is one in from the end of second row down, with her dark hair. There has always been speculation as to whether she had Mediterranean origins.

Another school photo, this time with eldest brother Herman, who emigrated from Holland after the war to pursue a peripatetic career in world banking.

A rare photo of the family all together. Hanny at the back on right. The professor admiring his wife; Maybe he is asking: 'Did we really produce this lot?'

Hanny facing camera and approaching her teen rebel years. Slightly disconnected, perhaps, from her friends?

She always wanted to look good, even if the farm didn't easily allow that to happen later. Younger sister Fred on the left.

The date of this is a mystery, but probably in Amsterdam before she left for Wales. Hanny looks confident, happy and blissfully unaware of the turn her life was about to take.

Newport High School first XV – 1937/8. Bob at 16 years old, on left hand end of middle row. He had just been selected for the Welsh Schools international rugby team. He signed up for war soon after, lying about his age.

Bob at home in Caerleon with his parents and sister-in-law, Betty, on signing up. His older brother Seymour had presumably already left. Mother Mabel forcing a smile, though father Archie looking more worried about the future.

Bob in the centre of his troop picture. He spent three years training in Scotland before joining the war in Italy.

Bob on the left, with his army pal Johnnie Bass. They only met once after the war, and never rekindled the relationship. Maybe looking back was too difficult. He threw all his medals away in a fit one day.

Bob (on the right) after the war, enjoying life playing cricket for Caerleon, before the big decision about where his future might lie.

Bob on his horse Anita, probably when he was living with his sister and travelling to the Rhadyr Agricultural College, having decided (despite family pressure to join Yardley's), to be a farmer.

November 1946 – Bob in the centre of the photo, at Rhaydr college. To his right is Trefor Moseley who took the spare room at Persondy, with Liz (in the back row above Bob) on free board and rent but with management duties.

The wedding party takes its stately route through the Vondelpark. Bob was well out of his comfort zone.

Hanny's parents at the wedding, with Bob's sister Mary alongside them. Bob's sister-in-law, Betty, also attended – making only three non-Dutch in attendance.

Cutting the cake. Bob hadn't tried on his hired shirt or suit before, and both were far too big. He had help to safety pin the pleats at the back of the jacket, and pin the sleeves up inside the arms.

Outside the church, after the ceremony. Hanny's sister Fred on far left. Her school friend alongside. Bob's nerves calming.

Hanny telephoning an old boyfriend with the good news.

Individual placeholders were made for all dinner guests, on which a picture of Persondy was painted. This one was made for Hanny's younger brother Arnold. The menu hinted that times were still austere.

The 'alien card' (as Hanny called it) was a 'Certificate of Registration' under the 1953 Alien Act. All foreigners had to be traced on a regular basis. Hanny never gave up her Dutch nationality, so never got a vote, or entitlement to state pension.

Life starts on the farm. They had a tractor, but no car. Bob used to drive it across the mountain, with Hanny in the link box, and drop her off outside Pontypool to go shopping.

Calf rustling was not her favourite job. She always had a fear of cattle and horses.

Haymaking time was a dear memory for Hanny. Here she is with Bob in the middle of bale hauling.

The only trip made to Wales by her father, this one a day's outing to the Kymin in Monmouth. Bob clearly trying to impress in formal wear.

On the same trip, this is Professor Dooyeweerd looking down the hillside to Persondy, gallant in pantaloons and beret. Not sure what the locals made of that.

Hanny's girlfriends visited her soon after she moved. Bob hated them giggling together.

Back on the farm, Alan is finding his feet around the sheds. Chickens line up in the field behind.

Son Alan arrives. This is outside Schipol Airport on a trip financed by Hanny's parents.

Outside Mrs Davies's little shop in Mamheilad. Mrs Davies and 'foreigners' didn't go together very well.

29 January 1959 – Hanny's mother is aware of Jantien's impending birth and has decided to visit Wales. Ferry bookings obviously low at that time of year.

Jantien ('Jant') appears. This shot is in the curious Victorian sash window of Persondy which Bob later replaced with a copy of the original 16th-century version.

Meal bags make great play sets.

The chicken houses were built from recycled materials – the bricks were all rejects from Little Mill brickworks, and soon suffered from frost damage.

Hanny with Alan and Jant, looking up towards the farm. Mynydd Garn Wen in the background. Things looking a little desolate.

Persondy from the west. One giant ash tree in the farmyard, but other trees thin on the ground. A world away from Oranje Nassaulaan.

All hands to the pumps at mucking-out time. Jant relishing the responsibility.

Jant and cousin Saskia outside the barn. For once everything is looking reasonably clean. Maybe because the Dutch relatives were visiting.

The family around 1970. Bob's sartorial elegance still clearly on view.

Three hundred and fifty pigs all contained on 1.5 acres around the house was never going to help create a bucolic image.

But if things were a little raw outside, the Christmas turkey could still be a thing of beauty.

Bob and Hanny, probably around 1980, outside the barn. The farm days starting to come to an end.

The Dooyeweerd reunion, 1988. Back row: Evelien, Hanny, Fred & Tineke. Front row: Johan (Joop) and Arnold, with special helper between. Herman, Mieke and Marja missing.

Bob working on some joinery project, probably a clock or piece of furniture. He'd have borrowed the timber from somewhere else.

Bob and Hanny, with the gardens now clearly taking shape.

At his happiest – Bob in the splendour of his garden. The pigs had rotavated the soil perfectly.

And in the main barn – not a pig or cow to be seen, just a handmade snooker table. Only he knew the secret line to the pocket.

Tineke, Hanny and Fred in a rare Amsterdam get together.

Hanny never lost her love of cycling. This is her in her 70s.

Their surprise 40th wedding anniversary. Bob's dress sense never left him.

Hanny at 70, still looking glamorous.

A special Amsterdam trip for Hanny's 80th, in 2016. This shot with Alan and Jant outside Oranje Nassaulaan 13. She never slept the whole trip and was the last one out of the bar every night.

Persondy living room interior after restoration. Bob's homemade Welsh dresser taking centre stage. The ceiling timberwork showing why it is such a special building.

And this is what Bob and Hanny created – Persondy's gardens

the passenger seat. We used the car for a while ourselves until we had yet another bit of luck – a phone call from Mr Pugh at County Hall, offering us another taxi contract, which some other firm was unable to carry out.

Another driver? We heard that Tom Wheeler, who used to work for Bob before we were married, was out of work at the time, and he was very willing to help us out.

These days you have to be checked by police if you are going to work with children, but that was not the case years ago. I was checked twice after the year 2001 – when the new law came in – because at that time I was working for a year or two looking after old and infirm people.

We used our taxis to transport school children for two years. The contracts were not very profitable, so we decided instead to use our two buses for taxi work in the evening to take people back and forth to parties. There was plenty of work about for that sort of thing.

We sold the 1800, but kept Herman's car. We did this evening work in turn; Bob would go one evening, I would go the next time. This paid fairly well; it all depended who the people in the party were. It certainly helped if everyone had consumed a lot of alcohol, so that when the hat came around for a tip for the driver they tended to lose their inhibitions.

But I hated this work. The money was good, but we inevitably had to wait for ages for people who were having a good time and didn't want to leave their parties. Then we had to get up early the next morning to do the school runs, and then the 'swill' run, feeding the pigs, cleaning the bins, then the afternoon school run. We were exhausted.

We lasted a year with the evening taxi work, but found it was getting too much – what with the school runs during the day, up at six in the morning, and keeping the pigs, which by now were filling the barn and one of the former chicken houses. And we had to collect the waste to feed the pigs. Everything had a time slot then. School run, then the first 'swill' run, clean all the bins, feed the pigs before the afternoon school run – then clean bins again, feed the pigs again, feed the family, collapse.

Anyone would think that during those years, when we were so very busy, there was not much time left for Al and Jant. Well, I can assure you that our two wonderful children made their own lives.

We never managed to get a contract to carry pupils to their school, which was Croesyceiliog Grammar, so they were picked up every morning and afternoon by another minibus company.

Our children differed widely. Alan very much enjoyed school but Jant did not. However, they both finished their schooling with excellent A-level results. During his school years Al made friends with a group of boys who were, like him, dreaming of making it in the world of pop music.

The Beatles were always top of their choice of music. Around Al's fifth year in school they had started a band consisting of drums, electric guitars, keyboard and a singer. They practised here in our living room most of the time. Because we lived in the countryside they would not annoy anybody with the very loud sound they produced. Except us!

I used to think they were great (of course), but was quietly getting concerned that Al was spending more time with the band than studying for his A-levels.

Well, after some time they managed to get an agent, who found a few gigs for them. One was all the way in Bristol, the others were closer to home, some in workingmen's clubs up and down the Valleys.

They had quite a lot of equipment between them, so how would they transport it all? Well, we had a van to transport the food waste (swill) from schools to the farm here. Al had learned to drive, so we decided that the band could use the van in the evening when we did not use it. After school Al set about scrubbing the van out and, after a few good squirts of aftershave, all was all ready to go.

They had a following on the road: Jant and her friends from school. They were called the roadies, and they carried in some items so that they never needed to pay to get in.

Bob and I did go to a gig in Cwmbran once. We arrived halfway through the performance in this smoke-filled and beer-saturated club, and loved the music they made and the applause they earned.

There was only one problem. The band, which went by the name of Train (later they changed it to Syn), only knew a handful of numbers, so they had to repeat their stuff time and time again. And when it came to 'request time' – well, you can imagine the rest.

But they did their thing, really enjoyed themselves and quietly disappeared into the mists of time when life became more serious. Al went to Oxford Polytechnic to study architecture.

Another thing Al enjoyed very much during his time in school was rugby. He carried on playing the game during the years spent in Oxford, and later on in London at London Welsh. He also played with the Abergavenny and Blaenavon clubs, and he followed Bob in his love of Pontypool RFC. At one stage, later in life, he and a small group got together to keep that club going through dire financial circumstances. As I write they are thriving, which Bob would have loved.

When Jant finished her A-levels she was too young to go to university (that was always what Bob wanted her to do, but not Jant!). So, being particularly good at drawing, she decided to apply to an art college in Newport. There she took a foundation course in art, and absolutely loved it. She then went on to teacher training college for art.

She had a friend here in the village, called Sara, who also went to the same college. During that year Jant turned into a hippy, and was often seen walking home from the ICI factory – after getting off the bus from Newport – in bare feet, wearing her Afghan coat, and with masses of curly long hair flying behind her. It was no wonder that she attracted the attention of anyone passing her on the way home.

She also used to wear this Afghan coat inside out, to get the woolly mammoth look to complete the picture. She would also be smoking a cigarette. She had a number of boyfriends, and really enjoyed life to the full. It was a boy named Jeffery from Caerphilly who changed the way she was thinking about life, just a little.

After she finished art college Jant used to go off every morning and stay away all day, together with Sara. They went everywhere by bus, as it was free for students, but time and again they would miss the last bus home, and I ended up going to pick them both up in our bus. It's a very long way from Mamheilad to Caerphilly, so the two girls eventually decided to stay over.

One day Jant asked if she could borrow my swimsuit – but it was not to go swimming in. Bob overheard our conversation, and incredibly he immediately realised what the swimsuit was going to be for. I still had no idea.

Jant and Jeffery had become involved with the Pentecostal Church, and Jant was so deeply impressed with this sort of religion that she wanted to be baptised there, hence the swimsuit. Jant had never told us anything about all this, so it came a bit as a bolt out of the blue.

We did not agree with any of this, and made straight for the church in question where Bob gave the vicar a pretty uncensored piece of his mind. With that, the episode was closed.

But it seemed to have started Jant on a religious path. Now she is very much involved in the running of the Baptist chapel where she lives. So it was a story which began badly and ended well.

Jant spent the last year or two of her teens working in Tesco supermarket, in between college terms, and later very near us here, in the Star pub in Mamheilad. A beautiful barmaid, she was spotted very soon by one of the regulars who became her husband.

During that time she was already taking commissions for paintings and drawings of people and places, something which she now makes a living from as an artist and tutor.

Bob and I have always been amazed at our children's talents, and even more at their drive and ambition to achieve what they set out to do in their lives.

Hard work and a good sense of humour are the only two things Bob and I might have instilled in them. They are quite important things, I think! The rest they did themselves.

*

Working life eventually ended for Bob and then for myself. We had worked so hard at various forms of farming to fulfil what Bob felt was his calling; we had taken our dwelling from something that was ramshackle and had few comforts into a beautiful historic home. Together we had given it everything.

All this work over the years kept us fit. We loved the outdoors. Of course we made errors but, rather than regretting, we moved on together. In the end, Ernie, our accountant with a company called Dorrell Oliver Ltd., told us that we had made more money from the buses than all our farming efforts. Ernie should know.

But we did the farming lark because we loved it, because it was just us together.

We made a mess of the whole thing but we didn't mind; we enjoyed the way our lives came round. I was very proud of Bob because he'd had such a difficult life during the war.

I suppose that it was also in some way born out of necessity as well. He was in the Army for eight years and that was a long time. He missed all his education when he was in the Army and, when he actually came back, everybody else, all his friends, well they had shot up the ladder and made a life for themselves professionally, whereas Bob was still struggling at the end of it and had to start all over again.

Al always used to tell us that we were not making any money, and asked us why we were living the way we did. Bob and I both said that it was enough for us. We were happy here and we didn't need more, we just didn't need it.

But it was the farming side, all the ups and downs,

that we loved the most and which was by far the most interesting. Not bad for a Dutch city girl from a six-storey Amsterdam house.

CHAPTER 8

Art of Broken Desks

BOB OFFICIALLY RETIRED at 65. That's when he drove one of our school buses for the final time. The toil on the land was behind him. But he was never one to sit still. He filled his days with repairing things, usually everyday things like chairs or an odd table. Our friends brought him broken furniture and a range of other stuff which he repaired for a small (very small) sum.

Even during our last period of farming and driving buses, he had already made wall-clocks, Welsh dressers for china (he made two for us, one for the kitchen and one for our living room), and later on he made one for Jant and one for Alan. He made a corner cupboard, a chest for my sewing, and a blanket chest.

All these items were made out of used wood which came from old school desks, which in those days were always made from hard wood.

These broken desks would always be put out with the rubbish at the schools where we picked up the swill for our pigs.

But Bob's pièce de résistance was his snooker table, which was full size. He sent away for a drawing of all the correct sizes and fittings. In fact he built two. The first one with a wooden base, which warped and made hitting accurate shots quite demanding! He gave that one away, and then built a second one with a proper slate bed which I remember was quite an undertaking to get. He sent away for the cues and balls and the green baize.

But the nets for the six pockets were home-made from the plastic nets used to hold oranges. He made circles of wire from which to hang the nets.

All his projects, large and small, became more than a hobby. They bordered on an obsession. He loved challenges and thoroughly enjoyed himself, spending hundreds and hundreds of hours sawing, hammering and chiselling in his workshop, surrounded in a cloud of sawdust.

His other love and interest was the garden. When we finished farming we hired a man with a bulldozer, who flattened out the top garden. We had a lovely large flat area where there could be ball games. Alan used to call the piece of ground Wembley when he was a little lad. At that time he was more interested in football than rugby, and the name stuck.

The Wembley part was much higher than the rest of our ground at the back of the barn, thus giving us a two-level garden area.

The piggery, hay barn and chicken houses were all demolished, leaving one wall standing which was part of the pigsties. Later that wall became part of my veggie garden, which was one of my joys.

Bob had really good insight when we tried to work out what to do with this big area. He decided to make gardens out of two-thirds of the whole area that he flattened. We bought a few trees and plants and, with many cuttings from other people, Bob created a beautiful garden that looked better and more beautiful every year. He had green fingers and the herbaceous borders were wonderful. He loved nothing better than pottering in the flowerbeds, then sitting with me under the willow tree at the garden table to enjoy a cuppa and just look at his wonderful creations.

*

In 1995 my dear Bob became ill. He had started having breathing difficulties which prevented him from doing the work he loved, which was a deeply painful thing. He started to stay indoors more and more which was so unlike him, and he began to pass a lot of his time reading.

Then his circulation became poor and he was advised to go for a short walk every day. But, gradually, even that became too laborious. Problems with his cerebellum were diagnosed. This is situated at the back of the brain and it controls balance.

Ultimately, there was no cure for this horrible complaint. He started to have increasing problems with his balance and, consequently, he fell over many times, sometimes hurting himself badly. Incredibly, he never broke anything, thank goodness!

But things just got worse. Bob was falling down so much that I could not leave him on his own. He just would not stay in a chair while I went to fetch something from outside. Once I was out of the house he would get up, and then immediately crash to the floor.

It really was such a heartbreaking time. Dr Gethin Jones, our local GP, advised that he should spend time in a local nursing home, to give me a break from caring. Such respite care for the carers themselves is now far more common.

Well, I tried to tell the doctor that it wasn't the best idea. I knew what would happen. But Bob went off anyway to the nursing home. It was just like fencing in a wild animal. Bob lost it completely and he had to come home after just a few days. I felt so desperately sorry for him. I loved him so much and this was not Bob at all.

As soon as he came home he calmed down straight away, and took to his favourite chair. It had an electric motor, which he would adjust from a sitting position to lying down at the touch of a button. That was a bonus.

Eventually, however, he had a series of small strokes and became completely housebound. He spent both his days and nights in his chair. He was unable to go upstairs or to move very much at all.

In the end, our doctor and district nurse managed to get us a proper hospital bed, and a contraption called 'lifting gear' – which only just got through the living room doorway – was delivered.

We put the bed in the living room under the window that overlooks the fields. And that was where he stayed for a few more years, never moaning ever; but seemingly content with being home. Life fell into a sort of pattern, however sad the background to it all was.

I will always be so glad that I could look after him myself and still could share a bit of life with him. I loved and admired him even more than ever by this time. He was such a strong character, he just would not let go until his body totally gave up on him.

Bob died 26 May 2000. He was 78. I miss him badly today, 20 years on, and always will. Some people say that when a loved one dies, part of them dies too. I know exactly how part of me definitely died.

It was 45 years since the man with the eggs had knocked on the door.

*

Later on in life, I suppose, friends trickled away because we were friends in pairs, so to speak. When Bob was alive we had a great time when people would come around, though he was probably happier when we were on our own. But when he died things changed and it was really hard not to have that group of friends. It did become lonely.

Nearly a year after Bob died I was finally ready to do something else. Keeping busy was what helped me to accept that he had gone and that from then on it would be a different sort of life. No more farming or school buses.

As luck would have it, I took a phone call from Nurse Collier, our district nurse, who used to help me look after Bob every Tuesday. She suggested that I helped her to look after some of her patients who needed help with washing themselves in the morning and preparing breakfast.

I jumped at the chance, so she gave me a list of addresses where all these people lived. This was, of course, voluntary work. All I needed was an apron, rubber gloves, some Vaseline which Nurse Collier provided, and I was on my way.

I just grew to love the work. These people were really elderly men and women, mostly cheerful and loving. Although, one or two were very bad-tempered people – not surprising, as some had some really bad leg ulcers, for which there is no cure, even to this day.

What struck me was that they were all so trusting. They didn't know me and I had no qualifications of any sort to do this work. The district nurse knew that I had looked after Bob all those years, so was well capable. But they never complained.

The work gradually came to an end, as some of the patients ended up in care homes, others passed on, and I was not needed any more, sadly. It was very rewarding work, and it was also humbling listening to some of their amazing life stories.

But one thing led to another. A very good friend of mine, Brenda Harris, was working for Social Services at that time. She was looking for someone to help a man in Pontypool, Les Jones. He was caring for three men who all had mental and physical problems.

One was 18, another was 42 and the third was 52. The latter was the only one out of the three who could talk a little, depending on what mood he was in. Les studied theology part-time, so he had very little time to look after his 'lodgers'. We decided that I would come twice a week, collect the men from different day-centres in the afternoon, bring them back, then cook dinner for everyone in the house.

Les had two children, teenagers, who were at school during the day. After dinner I would take one or two of the patients for a walk, before putting them to bed. This was quite early, as they had to be up very early in the morning for the minibus that called to take them to their day-centres.

It was voluntary work again, although Les would give me a £20 note every now and again. They were a lovely family, very appreciative of anything I could do to help them, and I really warmed to these men more and more. I used to get a big hug from the youngest one every time I arrived. He would just call out, even though he could not frame any words.

I did this work for two years, until advised by my doctor to take it easier as my blood pressure was starting to give concern. The teenagers are all grown up now. Les's son went to Aberystwyth University, and his daughter is now living in a flat in Pontypool with her partner. Les is now a vicar in the Baptist church in Ebbw Vale.

They were truly lovely people, a real family including the three 'patients'. The youngest one, Barry, went to Ebbw Vale with Les; the middle one, Andrew, died a few years ago, aged 51. The third one ended up in a special home as he became more and more difficult to handle, with fits of temper caused by pure frustration. I felt very, very sorry for him.

But it helped me cope with the loss of Bob, and was one of those experiences which added to life. It was what I needed to take myself out of myself at a tough time.

After a few months I entered yet another little interlude in my life. A dear lady called Mrs Shackleton, who lived here in Mamheilad, fell ill after she had a bad fall.

Her family decided she should sell her bungalow behind the Star pub, not far from Persondy. She moved to Usk where she bought a small new house. She had recovered from her fall but needed some help with getting in and out of bed, dressing and bathing.

I knew her well already and her daughter asked me if I could help her with these tasks. She had meals brought to her door by a private firm, but breakfast was my job to make. She was a bright and lively Yorkshire lass and we had many a laugh together about the good old days. She had a stairlift fitted, so that was a really good help.

I used to go there every evening about 7.30 too. We would have a cup of tea and a talk. Then I would help her get undressed and into bed and then lock the front door on my way out.

I would take the key to the neighbour, who she could ring if she needed someone.

Money was never discussed and I never asked for any, but she used to hand me a little retainer every now and again.

She reached her early 90s and became more and more helpless. Her family lived in different parts of Britain, one branch outside London and another on the west coast of Wales. They decided to get round-the-clock care for her in a home in the south of England. That was where she died.

She was financially very well off and the care home was very luxurious, but it doesn't matter how well off you are, loneliness is a very sad thing. Such a difficult state, especially late in life. She used to phone me from the home, and we would still have a laugh, mostly at life itself, and the things she used to get up to in her youth. It was a contact that we both needed.

As I reached my 80s, I was very aware that our land and home had undergone so many improvements – the creation of the landscaping and lawned area that Bob and I loved so much, and the big change in the early 1990s when Alan and Helen decided to convert the old barn that stood next to Persondy, and which over the years had housed our cows, chickens, pigs and, in later years, had been Bob's 'entertainment centre', complete with snooker table and makeshift bar. Work started in 1991 and by 1993 my son and his family were living next to me. How things had changed – I had joined my darling husband at Persondy when it was a ramshackle subsistence farm set in bleak, treeless, windswept countryside. But, between us, we have created something wonderful – a beautiful restored historic home and with the farmyard detritus replaced by abundant lawns and gardens. It is very special and a lasting tribute to our time together.

Part II

Alan and Jantien's
Memories of their Parents

CHAPTER 9

Freedom, Ghosts and Pig Swill

Life with Hanny and Bob (Mam and Dad)

Jantien Powell (née Francis)

Pigs are out!

The call 'Pigs are out' is one of my strongest memories of home. Mam would be cooking in the kitchen with the radio on. I was probably making crafts or drawing at the kitchen table. Al was probably listening to music.

The front door would crash open and Dad would bellow, 'Pigs are out', and we would all have to down tools instantly, don wellies and try to round up about 12 pigs that were hell-bent on freedom.

Dad would give us a rusty old bent tin sheet each and shout, 'Don't let them get past'. But I knew that I was no match for those bloody pigs. He would position me in what was possibly the easiest place, funnelling the pigs back into the shed. But as soon as they got their snouts under my tin sheet, they would lift it and fling it as if it were a feather and they'd be off again.

Dad would shout. We'd all groan. Mam would probably mourn her cakes burning in the oven, and we'd start all over again.

Annual bath

This event was a source of much amusement to my brother and I. Dad hated washing as much as any ten-year-old boy, and Mam would spend days building up to the job of forcing him into the bath. It must have been so frustrating for her as she really wanted everything in the house to run exactly as she planned it.

After she had eventually persuaded Dad to go and have a bath (maybe she had to use bribery – withdrawal of favours? Who knows!) and he had come downstairs smelling of aftershave, she would race up to the bathroom to empty the bath (woman's work, after all) and we would hear her wail: 'He's done it again, the soap is still dry!'

He would've sat in the water for five minutes, then slapped on the aftershave and come back down to his chair by the fire. Poor Mam. Strangely, at the time I never thought it odd that Mam would go and empty the bath water – I don't think women's lib ever reached our house.

Bob's garden

In his later years, when Dad had retired and was feeling quite rich on his state pension, he took up gardening. The pigs had all gone and he was left with 1½ acres of extremely fertile land, the pigs having destroyed every last weed and fertilised the land well over their farming years.

He created two big lawns separated by banks and herbaceous borders, stone steps and a pergola. Every plant had been stolen as a cutting from someone else's garden and the many trees had been harvested from the woods on the mountain behind the house.

He would wander off in the morning and come home triumphantly at midday with a rooted sapling of birch. He had tremendous vision planting his garden. The herbaceous borders were the envy of all around and he would give cuttings and little plants away to everyone (except me, from whom he would guard them jealously). I was reduced to copying his tactics and stealing a cutting when he wasn't looking.

He would always want us to walk the gardens with him as soon as we arrived. He absolutely loved his garden and would sit at the table under the pear tree with his coffee and survey all that he had created.

In the summer we would play badminton on Wembley, using the washing line as a net. Dad would umpire and bend the rules however he wished as we played for a championship with the local lads.

Mam would play and provide cold drinks and cakes. Bliss.

Liberation?

Mam was a very complex lady with a lot of conflicting ideas. She was extremely anti-women's liberation. Her views were that all women should stay home and look after their husbands, yet she worked out on the farm beside Dad every day.

When they came in for lunch or dinner, Dad would sit in his chair and ponder on life and she would cook wonderful meals, always with homemade cakes and puddings, clean the house, and do all of the paperwork. She was perfectly happy with this arrangement.

In later life she was very disappointed with the fact that I refused to get up at 4.30am to make a lunchbox for my husband to go on an early shift. She would also frown and say that I wasn't doing my job when I wouldn't cook him a meal when he arrived home from work at 10.30pm from the afternoon shift.

She thought all men should be welcomed home with their pipe and slippers, and tea on the table. Every man's dream really, wasn't she? As for her grandson-in-law, she called him 'poor Rich' and constantly berated my daughter on her inability to be a 'good wife'. Poor Rich is having to cook the tea tonight. Poor Rich is getting the washing in off the line.

The one thing Mam did insist on every morning was spending an hour in the bathroom, from whence she would emerge every single day of the year looking like a Hollywood star. It didn't matter if she was spending the day mucking out pigs, she was, for every hour of the day, the most glamorous woman in the county.

The Dutchees

I remember our house as always having visitors, which is strangely different to Al's memories. The local boys were always there 'helping' – probably gazing at Mam, who would work the farm in the summer in a bikini top and shorts, looking like a film star.

Various 'farmy-type' people called for coffee, sometimes

Dad's mates Ed and Trevor. But mainly, in my memory, every summer and every Christmas the house would fill with Dutch visitors from her enormous family.

Mam was absolutely in her element, arranging wall-to-wall mattresses for all the kids and extra beds in every room (Al and I were always relegated to the thinnest mattresses in the draughtiest corners). Carloads of family would arrive, pile into the house, and for the next fortnight the house was filled with the Dutch language.

Amazingly, Dad also loved all of Mam's family, though he was extremely relieved when they all went home and he could get back to his chair and his book. Alan and I would face-off the cousins as they arrived, just like Western gunslingers, and we would eye each other up and wonder how the hell we were going to get on with these kids we didn't understand, but within an hour we would be playing together, never minding the language barrier.

I am still very close to all of my cousins in the Netherlands and they and their children visit us and I see the same wonderful phenomenon of different languages mixing, even lately with my own grandchildren and theirs. What a lovely legacy you left, Mam.

At 'Dutchees' time Mam would be tireless. Up first thing making a full Welsh breakfast for 15, advising them on suitable walks, games, places to sit with a book etc., while she went outside and did the work of two men for three hours. Then back in to make a huge farmhouse lunch for everyone (something that we now always refer to as an 'Oma lunch') with homemade cakes to follow.

Then back out to work for the afternoon before returning for the same routine in the evening.

I remember long evenings with lots of wine (which was

always homemade and extremely potent!), endless stories (which we didn't understand because they were in Dutch), lots of laughing, bed at midnight and the same thing all over again the next day.

She was tireless and utterly loved these times. Some days she had time to come for a walk with the visitors and she would run up the mountain and jump over fences and berate everyone for being so slow. 'I don't know what's the matter with them,' she would say to me, 'they just can't keep up'. Treasured memories of a wonderful time.

Freedom

Every few years, when Dad could spare Mam from the farm, we would go to Holland to see the family. Dad would drive us to catch the boat train and we would board the ferry at Harwich to go to Hoek van Holland. Dad would probably return to his favourite place – home – with an illicit bar of chocolate (Mam was very health conscious and didn't have chocolate in the house).

The ferry was very exciting but I remember that Mam gave us complete freedom to run around the decks and explore, and she never seemed to worry about safety at all.

The same freedom applied at home for my wonderful childhood, complete freedom to roam the woods and fields with absolutely no chores expected of me – ever! At lunchtime in the summer Mam would ring a big old school bell and we would hear it wherever we were and race home for dinner. She didn't worry about us at all, which may have been a result of her upbringing in Amsterdam where she had little attention from her parents. However, for us it was a wonderful childhood and it taught us to look after ourselves!

119

Parties

Mam had such strong ties to her family, most of whom lived in Holland, but some had moved elsewhere – Canada and California. They stayed in close contact throughout her life, and her nieces and nephews and their children, in turn, came to stay with her.

They are a very special family, very creative, musical and hugely talented. Every special occasion would see the family turn up with all their musical instruments which would have been piled into their cars and driven across. The family choir would sing specially written songs to mark occasions such as birthdays, wedding anniversaries etc.

Mam so loved a party, she would dance all night. My latest memory of this is my sixtieth birthday party in 2019. Mam danced non-stop with all of her great-nieces and nephews and her grandchildren and great-grandchildren; her face lit up with happiness.

Even when she was 83 years old she could drink us all under the table and never had a hangover, and was then always up early for breakfast. She was an amazing woman of two worlds, a tough and hardworking farmer's wife and, when the occasion arose, she would crack open the wine, put on the high heels and glamour and dance the night away. She was a knockout.

Shoe

I remember one Christmas Aunty Fred, Mam's closest sister, and her family came to stay and we ended up playing a ridiculous Dutch game called 'pass the shoe' on the living room floor in front of the fire.

Mam and Aunty Fred laughed so much that they had

to change their knickers three times as they kept wetting themselves. Then we had to stop playing as they had run out of clean knickers. Dad carried on reading his book in his chair, quietly chuckling. He always said it was 'stupid' but his quiet smile and little chuckles belied his words.

Meeting Rich

The first time Mam met Rich (my daughter Tiz's now husband) was at her seventieth birthday party which was held at the Lamb & Fox pub in Blaenavon. She had already downed a fair few glasses of wine, surrounded by her Dutch family (who all came over for every occasion), and was in high spirits.

She spotted Tiz and Rich arriving and shouted 'what a hunk!' She hurried to introduce herself by sitting on his lap. He was 28 and she was 70, and she greeted him with, 'Hi, I'm Jant's mam. If you ever get fed up of Tiz, I'm here!' She was ridiculous and lovely, amazing and brave.

Legs

I met someone recently that Mam had driven to school for years on the minibus. He told me that he always wanted to sit in the front seat so that he could look at her legs.

Ghosts

When Al and I were little, Mam would tell us about the monk that would stand by her bedside in the night and look at her. He 'visited' for many years and eventually she would say, 'It's alright, he just stands and looks, then he goes'. The last time she saw the monk, instead of just standing and watching her he walked across the room to the old fireplace, which had just been uncovered by Dad.

He stooped down, picked up a parcel from within the fireplace, and left. She never saw him again after that, though she continued to see various 'spooks' during the nights for the rest of her life. She was very philosophical about it, but I as a child was terrified! It was a strange thing to share with your child. She gave us detailed descriptions of her ghosts whenever she saw them. I wonder why she didn't think that it might scare me, and why I never felt able to tell her that it did. I would bury myself in my quilt and be terrified of the monster under the bed and all of Mam's spooks!

Ridiculously, in later years, when Mam was away and I went to stay at Persondy with my husband and my brother and his wife, none of us would go into the house alone – we were scared!

I have since discovered something called hypnopompic hallucinations which cause visual, tactile and auditory events during the transition from sleep to wakefulness. People report hearing voices, feeling phantom sensations and seeing people or objects in their rooms. I am sure Mam had this condition. In her last days, when we were caring for her in our house, she woke one morning, came into our kitchen and complained that she had been trapped in her room for hours because of all the people having a party in the house! As this was during the 2020 Covid-19 lockdown, it was very strange!

She would wake in the middle of the night, put on the light and wake Dad to show him the monk who was at the bottom of the bed, watching from within a dark hood. (Mam once described the appartition to a local historian who congratulated her on accurately describing an Elizabethan tenant of the house – spooky! Dad never saw him of course, and was very grumpy at being woken up, and told her to go back to sleep. Once, Dad told me that she woke him in the middle of the night and stripped the bed, much to his annoyance, looking for the top of the mustard pot. Oh well, I suppose it couldn't always be a spooky monk!

Sunday tea

When we were kids Mam was very strict about all meals being eaten at the kitchen table. We couldn't leave the table until after pudding, except for Dad. Every evening he would mutter 'must check the fire' and disappear into the living room with his pudding to watch telly. My husband still practises the same behaviour.

But Sunday tea was special. Taken in front of the fire in the living room, I remember that it was always sardines on toast followed by peaches with Ideal Milk. Then everyone had to watch Mam's choice of Sunday serial, *Upstairs, Downstairs* through to *The Onedin Line* and countless others.

My own children have fond memories of Sunday tea at Oma and Opa's house (Dutch for grandma and granddad) every week when they were young.

Alan never liked the lifestyle at home and his memories are very different to mine. He hankered after a city life and couldn't wait to leave, while I loved the whole 'make do and mend' bit and the solitude of the mountains and the canal. I would walk for miles on the canal bank and sit on a bridge with my book, or spend days sewing or painting at home.

Mam and Dad were quietly supportive, never actually sitting and doing anything with me, but Dad would always critique my paintings, usually pointing out faults and telling me to try again. 'There's no such word as can't,' he would always tell me. 'Try harder.'

And he built me easels and a quilting frame, and they let me mess up the whole house making stuff. His advice has stood me in good stead. I say the same words to my grandchildren.

Like swallows, Alan and I would return to home as a place of peace and refuge.

Swill

When I was 18 or 19 Dad developed blood poisoning in his right arm, a huge lump of infection appeared overnight. He would clean out the drains by rolling up his sleeve and plunging his arm down the hole – so it was no surprise. He was confined to the armchair for a few weeks and I had to leave art college for the duration and run the pig farm with Mam.

The 'swill run' was one of the jobs we had to take over. So there we were, a teenager and a super model in a rusty old transit van held together with string, driving around all of the schools to collect dustbins full of kitchen waste to feed the pigs.

Those bins were really heavy!

The dinner ladies would fill them right to the brim, quite often with liquid food, and we had to lift them on to the back of the transit. Mam would say 'back straight, bum out 1, 2, 3' and we did it all. Sometimes 20 bins in two journeys. We would get the giggles occasionally and then it was virtually impossible to lift anything!

Once, the van broke down at a busy traffic lights and refused to start, and I can see Mam's horrified face now as

I leisurely ambled off in my filthy clothes to ask a smartly-dressed policeman with white gloves to give us a push. Poor man. He did it though!

Alan learnt to drive in the swill van, and I remember going with him and Dad on the swill run one day, with Alan driving. Pulling up on a hill approaching a small roundabout, Al had to practise his hill start, and failed spectacularly! Jerking on the handbrake as the van began to roll backwards, a heavy bin of swill began to slide to the back of the van ominously. It burst through the back doors – which were only ever fastened with binder twine – and deposited its load of school dinners on the road!

Muttering under his breath, Dad got out, saying, 'C'mon kids, let's clean it up.' He and I had to scoop up the swill back into the bin as best we could and place it in the van, tying the doors shut.

Where was Al? Hiding under the steering wheel for fear that someone might see him. Different aspirations, see.

CHAPTER 10

Dad

Alan Francis

When the largest weaner ran through Dad's legs, I was just able to catch it. It had nowhere to go as we had barricaded the gap between the sheds and the market trailer, but that didn't make catching it any easier. It was slippery too from all the mud and pig shit around the place.

It was a bit like a comic circus / tag / mud-wrestling act. Me and Dad against a line of young porkers. We'd line up facing each other at the start and then, tin sheets at the ready, we'd advance; separate one of them into a corner hard against the brick and concrete block walls of the outbuildings, and in a sea of shouting and shit eventually hoist it up into the end of the trailer.

We laughed quite a bit as we did it, which all helped. Dad knew he wasn't getting any younger, what with the 40 a day he used to do as well, so it was good to have me around.

Dad had no obvious interest in money and spent little time on paperwork, leaving Mam to do the figures and the grovelling letters to the Ministry or the Inland Revenue.

But he was a farmer, independent and proud, and if it had to be pigs then so be it.

But a pig farmer is a curious thing. You don't roam the hills or spend your days on a tractor, and don't do the things most farmers do. So it was a lonely existence. Dad and Mam had each other, me and my sister, a dog or two, a rickety old van on its last legs, the house, the sheds, the pigs, and that's about it.

Our pig period was a grimy one, but it's hard to make an intensive pig breeding factory look faintly romantic, green or even agricultural. There were 300 porkers on only one-and-half acres surrounding our house. There wasn't a blade of grass to be seen, just lots and lots of shit.

Buy in some weaners, fatten them up on waste school dinners, do the tag wrestling bit, and then wait for the cheque. It was an odd routine and the occasional sale would bring in some funds and then we'd eke it all out, shovelling shit, till next time.

It didn't start off that way and, thank God, it didn't finish up that way either.

*

Dad pulled me up. I wasn't doing it right. 'You're like a bloody lion, son – a dandelion.' He could do really incredible things in those days, like pick me fully up off the ground with one arm, but I was lean and slim-chested, and muscles had yet to be properly developed. He was all dark eyes, thick brown arms and no neck. Fingers like pork sausages. He could haul bales all day and the strings never blistered him.

*

I bowed down low waiting for his first swipe, ready with a proper defence like Cassius Clay. But he was all aggression, low and stooping, and even if I tried to launch myself at him, I had to back away from his sheer strength and physicality. I would wait for my moment, poised liked a viper, but one step forward by him and I'd be back under the kitchen table.

He'd laugh, straighten up to check what Mam had cooking, and I'd jump on his back to show him I wasn't finished. The pewter pots hanging from the low oak beams would fall again as my moptop caught them. Considering their supposed antique value, they looked a bit knocked about to me. A few more dents wouldn't make any difference.

Dad loved home. 'He'd build a moat around us if he could,' Mam would say, 'and pull up the drawbridge for most of the year.' Everyone loved him. He was a reasonably big man, without ever being enormous, but, in rare public appearances, very aloof and reserved. Newport High School, see. The Francis connection with Yardley cosmetics, all 'Britishness' and public school, but with enough of an independent streak to stay in Wales and, of all things, to be a farmer.

Aunty Mary was a farmer too, but it was different. She had a farm and it looked and smelled like a farm, and she talked all horsey. Uncle Seymour, Dad's brother, worked for Yardley cosmetics, smoked a pipe and sat in his armchair reading the *Telegraph* and smelling of money. Dad smelled of pig shit and Woodbines, and read Harold Robbins. It was a bit different.

If no-one ever visited, it might have partly been because we never went out. We couldn't afford to go out, so we didn't. And when we did, Dad had an unshakeable belief in his superiority over everyone else, whilst at the same time donning his checked shirt full of stains and belting up his trousers with binder twine. Mam's patience persevered, though his lack of interest in personal hygiene mystified her. My sister Jant and I would repeat the mantra: 'Had your yearly bath yet, Dad?' We'd all be in fits.

Dad was also an artist. In fact, he was a kind of mix between craftsman and architect, though never to the point of precise detail. One day he drew a picture. I'd never seen him do that before and it was good. Not OK, actually quite good. Out of his head and immediate. With a pencil. A sketch. It had depth, tone and detail. He never did it again, but he clearly had it in him.

Before the Second World War changed his life he did an apprenticeship at Burgess Architects in Cardiff. His fondest memory was taking an age to draw a very exquisite north point on a plan.

His later creative work lacked that attention to the minutiae, but he could certainly create things out of nothing. In the beginning bits of left-over wood became wall clocks, complete with cheap battery powered workings. Later he got carried away, one day dismantling the sixteenth-century turkey oak wall plates from our stone barn to turn them deftly into a full size, accurate Welsh dresser.

He'd sit there in his 'shed' night after night, in an enormous and growing pile of sawdust, with one light bulb hanging off its wiring, turning some detailed doorknob for a chest of drawers. And then he'd give it away a month later.

He built a full-sized snooker table once, complete with a warped timber base, as slate was out of the question, and only he knew the secret line to the pocket. That table went for free, too. Someone up the Garn that I'd never heard of, but he needed it. He did build a second table later, this time with a slate bed he'd acquired when Pontypool Pool Hall was closed down. But it wasn't the same really. No mystery in the shots.

*

The History Society Visit to Persondy (c.1985)

I sat patiently waiting for them to arrive. There were loads more than I expected. A curious party of middle- and old-aged oddities. The History Society. Balding worried-looking old biddies, and they were definitely Usk rather than Ebbw Vale. They tapped on the oak-panelled walls as they walked round, marvelling at the beauty. They hadn't realised it had been in a derelict state before granddad took it on. Full of sheep! Can you believe it! And one whole side of the house had collapsed! Well I never!

Mam was brilliant at the host bit. Tea and Welsh cakes at the ready, she'd do a great impersonation of the *Antiques Roadshow* mixed with *Historic Houses*. The visitors gingerly opened the latched and braced timber door Dad had added to keep out the draughts, and carefully made their way up the solid stone semi-circular stair built in the thickness of the sixteenth-century walls.

One of them grabbed the newel post to steady himself as he climbed, breaking into joy at the marvel of sixteenth-century workmanship that created it and the post and panel balustrade at its head. They all nodded in agreement. Mam and Dad nodded too, which was a bit odd I thought, because I could distinctly remember Dad making all that not long before.

Not only that, but from timber nicked from the listed building next door. Dad winked at me and Mam barely hid a crooked smile. So the great know-it-all bunch didn't quite know it all after all. I sat quietly, but Dad never let on.

*

He was great at that, once sitting listening for an age to our pompous old vicar droning on about his exploits on the rugby field as a kid. I longed to butt in. But, you old git, don't you know my dad played for Wales? Dad didn't mind at all. In fact, better not to say. He'd prefer the clown carry on. Dad was probably dreaming of some Harold Robbins scene anyway. Never too good at listening was Dad.

Mind you, as I've mentioned religion, he was an expert in the redistribution of wealth. Maybe it's a bit like continuous summers when you're young, but I seemed to remember being out and about with him a lot.

Not visiting anyone of course, and not venturing very far, but we'd toddle along in the Land Rover, him pom-pomming away, picking up a newspaper, looking out for the best houses and then, all of a sudden, he'd reverse into some lay-by. Out we'd both get, shovels at the ready, and in ten minutes we'd have the council's entire gravel pile in the back. Took them quite a while to mend the road usually, but Dad's new sheds came on a treat!

For many years I thought that's where building materials came from. It never dawned on me that there'd been no exchange of cash. Whole sand piles shifted mysteriously, and then we'd jump back in and he'd pom-pom his way home.

It was possibly the only thing he shared with his brother, that pom-pom thing. Best practised with your mind totally elsewhere. Puff out your cheeks and do a Louis Armstrong impression without the trumpet.

We hardly ever went on family trips. When I was young I never went to Cardiff. Why would I? It was quite a long way away with only the tortuous A48 for access, and there was nothing there for me, I suppose. Shops of course, though probably a pretty poor selection in those days. And restaurants, but I never went in one of those until a lot later.

The castle must have been considered because we took our Dutch relatives to all the Welsh castles, one by one, every summer. But I suspect a castle in a city was a different thing altogether. And why would the Dutchees want to go to a city anyway?

'They all live in one already,' was quite a familiar response to cover up the more likely horrendous sense of fear that would engage Mam at the thought of driving and parking in a 'big' city like that. Dad didn't do much 'travelling'. Newport was a rare day out. Cardiff was the other side of the world.

Which is all the more curious because Dad was born there, and lived there in his early years. The Francises were originally a Vale of Glamorgan family. Dad came along on 16 March 1922 at Whitchurch Hospital, Cardiff, youngest by some way of three children gifted to Archibald and Mabel, who were probably of *decent class* due to granddad's association with the Yardley family of cosmetics fame.

Dad could posh it up with the best very easily. He spoke like a wartime BBC commentator. All his family worked for Yardley, including granddad. Great-uncle Tat was the king-pin apparently, and some kind of equity partner in the group, but I doubt much of the wealth got transferred to Archibald.

Later they left Cardiff, when Dad was still quite young, for the splendour of 'Litchfield' on the Ponthir Road in Caerleon, where Archibald would escape Mabel's evening rants by disappearing down to the Hanbury Arms with such regularity that forever after he was dismissed as a drunk.

It stopped Dad from imbibing for a great many years until, one day, he woke up and realised that Archibald was just having a few beers with the lads to escape the dreaded Mabel, and took to drink with great abandon thereafter.

We often drove past Litchfield, but never went in. I've thought of doing so since but something stopped me. It's a detached Victorian, or possibly Edwardian 'gentleman's residence'. Dad clearly admired it, and the black-and-white photos from his childhood show him either in his cricket whites, army clothes or casual dress, but the latter was always tweedy and upright. It was clearly a rigid upbringing, upper middle class and mowed lawns.

Not a big plot but neat and tidy and close enough to the railway station so that during breakfast he would wait to hear the train whistle as it turned Ponthir corner, and know that he still had time to race to the platform to get to school. I've sat on the Pontypool to Newport train many times since, and checked and timed it as it passes through Caerleon.

Either Dad was faster than Usain Bolt or the trains in those days cluttered along at five miles an hour. He wasn't full of stories from his youth. Perhaps they disappointed.

*

War

'Join the line Francis, and report to the registration desk over there.' It wasn't a quick line. It shuffled nervously full of raw youths, some just out of short trousers and some still in them. 'Name?' 'Francis.' Dad always pronounced the 'a' hard, like in 'apple', not 'all'. He always had trouble giving his name on the phone, especially to English people, and I'd hear him repeat himself often. They all said it that strange way as if they were French with a long 'a' and pronounced nasal twang, so perhaps they hadn't heard the Gwent version before.

'Public or state?' boomed the uniform refilling his quill. 'Public or state what?' replied Dad, never furiously quick off the mark. 'School of course!' Even louder this time. 'Don't know,' says Dad. Uncle Seymour would have known. So would Mary.

'Don't know? I've never heard such a thing!' The officers rolled around, guffawing.

'Well I suppose we can look it up.' The uniform starts turning the pages. Dad was 16. It hadn't been important. 'Newport High. Ah, here it is... ummmm... yes, public. Over there. Join that queue on the left.' It wasn't for quite a while that he learnt that that was the 'officers' queue. State boys went to the right – privates. He was nervous.

'Where are we going?' 'Not sure, but I don't think it's Cardiff,' says the boy next to him.

No, it wasn't. Far from Cardiff, in fact. Perth in western Scotland to be precise, via Glasgow. He was to be troop sergeant to a bunch of hardnosed Glaswegians at 16 years old: 31st Perth Royal Artillery anti-aircraft regiment.

Dad's war years are, to a certain extent, shrouded in mystery. He didn't return home for seven years. Really? I suppose that's possible. At the appropriate time, when training was complete, he was shipped from Perth to Italy through the Mediterranean, via North Africa, landing in Sicily where there was 'serious fighting', and then making his way across the mainland to Brindisi initially, then Naples and subsequently to fight in the Battle of Monte Cassino, one of the most important at that stage of the war. He even did a short stint on the other side of the Adriatic, fighting in Split, Yugoslavia. He was in charge of C troop. There were 40 men to a troop, with six sergeants. His troop had a Bofor gun. He had his own motorbike, later his own van, and was, I suspect, an independent young man in the flush of youth.

In later life, when Dad lay disabled for years on a makeshift bed in our living room, cared for by a devoted wife guilty at leaving him for a few days in the local County Hospital, I drew up a chair to his bed and started talking to him again about his wartime years. He had always fobbed me off in my youth. 'How many Germans did you kill, Dad?' 'Ooh, stacks, son. Piles of them on the end of my bayonet.'

He rarely discussed anything seriously, and certainly not the war. Never opened up for a second. Never joined in any national celebrations and turned the telly off when Remembrance Day was on the news. Out on the farm one day, he came across a dead pig with its guts spewing out.

He turned away from Mam and threw up in the corner, though he had never been squeamish before. 'Seen too much of that,' was his only comment.

For years we had a solid silver knife in the house with a swastika on the handle. Dad took it from a captured German. It's now somewhere down by the Tumpy Field gate. I dropped it climbing the tree there and never found it afterwards.

Most dads might have blown their top at my clumsiness, a rare military antique lost for ever. Dad didn't seem that bothered. Looked up when I told him, then put his head back in his book. I've often thought of taking a metal detector back there one day. The tree has gone now, but the stump remains in the hedge. I walk past it now and think about Dad every time.

But it was obviously a good day, that day by his bedside, and he was reasonably free-flowing, more than at any other time that I could remember. Army number 930015. Just like that. He didn't seem to have a clue what day it was, or even perhaps where we were, but he still remembered that. Extraordinary. Tattooed into his soul, and staying with him mentally till the end.

I wonder how much else. I picture the Battle of Monte Cassino as a constant wave of Nazi firepower reigning down from Monte Cassino and on to the Allies. Was there any respite? Was there a day, or even an hour, when everyone stopped firing? Dad was in a tent he said. A tent? In the middle of the battle? He woke up one morning, stepped outside and fell headlong into a massive bomb crater. Two feet to the right and he would have been wiped out. I've thought about that often.

And he also remembered, curiously, for he'd never

talked about it before, where he was when VE Day was declared. In France apparently, though the exact location escaped him. He had fought all the way through Italy, and forever after cherished the Italian way of life, its devotion to family, its sense of community.

He often mentioned the Sidoli fish and chip shop in town. How they'd come over after the war, and how close they were, though I'd never seen him speak to them once. Dad? Start talking to some Italian he didn't know? More chance of him engaging in protracted correspondence with the vicar.

He always said he had a fair smattering of Italian. I pressed him one day: 'Nienti faggies dans ma poche.' Yes, brilliant Dad. A fine concoction of Italian, French and slang English! Perhaps a chat-up line for the local girls looking for cigarettes?

But as for further detail, that's about it. A few photos taken in uniform somewhere overseas. Johnnie Bass was his best mate, and there's that photo of the two of them, against a low barbed wire fence in the field. Dad with cocked beret, and bolshy stance, smiling.

Johnnie Bass was a Jock, and the two met later, but only once I think. Although reports back were good, it was never repeated. Too difficult? Too many difficult memories? Too many colleagues lost? He did have a lot more memorabilia but, when I was young, threw a fit one evening and burnt the lot, despite protestations from Mam.

And even on that good day by his bedside, nothing more came out. The war went with him, and a good many more questions went with him, too. He wouldn't have minded in the slightest. Never questioned me as to why I wasn't more interested.

I was caught up in a scrap at the school dance once. Actually, I had nothing to do with it. I turned around from a joke with some pals, my denim jacket and jeans shining and over-long hair flying – to be met by a wall of local skinheads taking exception to my look. My pals ran for it but I was cornered and took a good kicking.

Dad picked me up later, as we'd arranged. I was fine but feeling a little sorry for myself. Dad thought the whole episode was 'stupid'. So did I, I said, but I'm not sure I could do anything about it. 'Stupid' muttered Dad under his breath, ignoring me, and we carried on home in silence.

I still have the original letter, written to Dad's mother Mabel in June 1940 – the dark days of the war – recommending Dad for promotion and stamped 'very urgent'. However, permission wasn't granted. And, interesting that it wasn't addressed to Granddad either, though he was still alive then, and even outlived her. Mabel ruled the roost I suspect. I know Dad was devoted to her, so maybe he gave her name as next of kin; Granddad never had that position I suspect.

And it's interesting that the war probably changed many things for Dad, like it did for almost everyone involved. He'd come from a middle-class family, and most probably (if his brother and sister were anything to go by) a Conservative-voting household. But Dad returned from the war an ardent Labour-voting socialist, and other than the occasional foray with the Liberal Democrats, stayed that way to the end. It was (and still is) a curious aspect of life for those smallholdings on the edge of the south Wales coalfield, that the local community was very mixed. Sure, you had Pontypool Park estate, some outright Tory farmers, the church- and chapel-goers, but you also had mining families, and 'workers' who held a job in town but lived in the countryside. The Griffiths family came to live on Mynydd Garn Wen just above Persondy at the same time as Granddad. They were communists. It was a diverse community and I know that Dad loved that. And although he could comfortably hold his own with the well-to-do, he preferred the company of Dai from the Mountain or a former miner, Ed Lewis, two local characters he spent a lot of time with. Did much of that come from his time in the Forces? Yes, I suspect so.

Manners

'Look son, just keep that bit of wood in the right position. You're moving it too much.' Dad kept building the wall. It needed to be finished and construction tolerances weren't important, but getting it done was. Something wasn't going right. Perhaps I wasn't concentrating. He berated me again. 'But I don't think it's going to work Dad, the bastard thing just isn't staying there.' Dad was crouching over the bricks, but he dropped his tools, kept his position and simply looked up at me. 'Don't you ever use words like that again.'

I froze. It's true, I'd never sworn in front of him before, but the words just tripped out accidently. In the Army he must have been drowned in cuss from start to finish, so why the big deal? But I didn't ever swear in front of him again, ever, and I don't recall him ever resorting to it, either.

Now that's a curious thing. Was it an Army thing after all? Officers supping their G&Ts and watching their Ps and Qs whilst the lads swore and whored their way around Europe? Not sure it was, but perhaps it was a class thing. Perhaps it was to do with Mabel. He obviously loved her a lot and with Archibald not around much and his siblings gone, perhaps she influenced his manners and attitude hugely. She was apparently a larger-than-life individual and from 'good English stock', so maybe certain habits stuck.

For Dad could, and did, mix it with the lads quite easily and preferred doing so.

Whilst he could easily act the country squire one minute, exchanging a horseback anecdote with Colonel Harry Llewelyn during a Monmouthshire Hunt outing, he was more at home in front of the telly with Trefor and Tom Wheeler watching Tommy Farr.

Did they swear together then? Perhaps, if I wasn't there, but I suspect not. I suspect it might have been a little different in those days if you had any notions or in-built belief in your class, and to Trefor or Tom, Dad was probably 'above' them, even if they laughed together.

Nowadays BBC commentators, pillars of industry and even, heaven forbid, the Royal family actually make a point of liberally punctuating whole statements with words previously banned from Radio 4, simply in order to add to their gravitas and 'whole-beingness'. They can, so they do. In Dad's day, if you swore you were working class, and he certainly wasn't. It's the Army thing, I've no doubt, but from a slightly different angle. The harshest he'd come out with was 'hell's bells and buckets of blood'. What was that? Shakespeare? Mickey Spillane? I'm not sure when the middle classes started to say 'fuck' in public, but it must either have been after Dad opted out of society or he was in some other parallel universe.

Is it about manners? Decorum? The great Pontypool second row John Perkins once told me that even though the air over Pontypool Park was the bluest imaginable when coach Ray Prosser was taking training, he would cut down any man in the clubhouse later who uttered even the faintest hint of bad language. The Park was Prosser's territory, but in the clubhouse, well that was different. And women might be there.

Did something similar apply with Dad?

Dad was driving home once, with me alongside. I think it was in one of our pig vans. We were on Folly Lane, close to our driveway, when another car sped down the lane towards us. The lane is too narrow for two cars to pass. Someone has to reverse. The other car was far closer to a passing point – our driveway as it happens – so we waited and gestured, but they didn't budge.

Dad knew everyone on our lane, and this wasn't one of them. It slowly dawned on him who they were. They were the Bradleys. They were related to the Williamses above us, and Dad, unusually for him, openly didn't like them, though I have no idea why. We waited, but there was nothing. No suggestion that they would move, or even acknowledge that someone needed to move.

After five minutes nothing had happened, just the two cars staring each other out in silence. Then, quite suddenly, Dad turned off his engine, got out of the car, and, calling me with him, started walking home, leaving the old pig van to block the dreaded Bradleys' way.

The two of us sauntered past them, Dad whistling merrily. He laughed. 'Well I've got all day; I wonder if they have?' Within a minute they started reversing. When we waved to them after we passed each other, they looked the other way.

Miserable buggers. I wonder if Old Man Bradley was

a war hero. Well he certainly wasn't doing well on the manners front. But, then again, few of the toffs ever did, and Dad hated that. He also wasn't going to let the old bugger get the better of him. They had obviously crossed swords before.

So it wasn't just a good manners thing, more a matter of pride and self-belief, especially when dealing with those who might be a little 'above you'. Returning home from work in London one weekend, I explained that I often felt very comfortable in the company of those clients who were clearly English Public School and, on the face of it, from a very different background to me.

Dad related to that straightaway. Not because we were, somehow, of similar breeding after all, but because the English couldn't place me. Was I public school or not? Dad got it. Perhaps a little bit of his demeanour had filtered down to me.

Sport

'Al! ... Al!' I was working at my drawing board in the Abergavenny office. I must have been intensely involved, as I hadn't heard his shout. My first-floor window overlooked busy Nevill Street, so perhaps Dad's shouts had been drowned out. He tried again. Louder this time. 'Al! ... Al!' Eventually I looked up, and there was Dad down on the street outside holding up the back page of the *Abergavenny Chronicle*.

We had won against our local rivals, The Garn (Garndiffaith RFC), and I'd been lucky enough to grab the headlines. I smiled and he laughed. He loved his rugby. Mam looked embarrassed. Not like Dad to shout across the street like that.

I don't think Dad saw that game, but I do remember him

watching Abergavenny play my old club Blaenavon at Bailey Park. I captained the side that day and there was a good crowd lining the touchlines. We were losing, and I was giving our pack a good dressing down, my speech littered with f'ing this and f'ing that as I tried to get us back into the game. I heard Dad's cries of anguish on the touchline and imagined him bemoaning my swearing to Mam.

But he would have loved the atmosphere nevertheless, and no doubt was proud that I was leading the side. He was talking about it to someone one day, and they had asked him whether he had ever played. He had replied 'not to the level of Abergavenny firsts'. Now that was odd. The *South Wales Argus* match report still hangs in our kitchen. Wales Schoolboys had drawn with England Schoolboys in Bristol and Dad had figured in the Welsh team at second row. He was only 6' 2" at his best, but I suspect that was enough to mark you out as a big bloke in those days. Yes, he had played for Wales. Did he think international schoolboy rugby not as hard as the Monmouthshire league?

'I timed it just right, son. He was a tall bloke but I hit him just right. Caught him right in the solar plexus just as he caught the ball. They had to carry him off. And right in front of the selectors.'

Yes, Dad's rugby days were a strong part of his teens, but this didn't carry on once the war started – maybe there was no rugby at his army camp in Scotland? But what did capture his imagination (or perhaps start to overtake rugby?) was boxing and cricket. He boxed for his regiment and was, for one match, an Army champion, though I don't recall at what level. During his first title defence his opponent broke Dad's nose so badly he never properly breathed through it again, but at least he had got to championship level. Although outwardly extremely calm, under it all Dad was fiercely competitive.

He loved his cricket too. Was a regular for Caerleon on his return from the war, and I remember him sitting in front of the telly at some point in the '60s, howling with glee when Colin Milburn hit an outrageous six against some touring team. In his later years, when he had crafted himself a full-size snooker table, he'd be out there every evening challenging his new son-in-law, Mam's home-made wine to hand, and happier than I'd ever seen him. Sport was huge for him, though it had never really floated Mam's boat, especially after her only venture to Cardiff Arms Park, when crammed into the South Enclosure (a gruesome standing experience for some in those days) the bloke behind her pissed over the back of her coat as it was too difficult to get out of the enclosure and the bogs were probably full anyway. She kept her humiliation to herself, but never joined Dad for a rugby international again.

The later years

'Well, that's spoilt our Christmas! Dad was fuming but, as ever, he hardly took it out on me at all – no swearing, no theatrics; just a certain calmness and a sudden freeze in communication. Mam got to know all about that near the end, but it hadn't happened that often for me, yet. I hadn't seen him coming, chatting away to my pal in the passenger seat. Maybe I wasn't even looking, but we met in a howl of grating steel on the corner of Croes y Pant lane; me driving Mam's minibus and Dad in his.

Getting the vehicles road-worthy was never top of Dad's lists and, anyway, that sort of thing cost money – so no doubt the brakes on both vehicles were a bit dodgy. Dad and posh cars never went together very well.

*

The minibuses forged a big change in Mam and Dad's world. Well, there was Mam, a central Amsterdam girl now residing on a subsistence hill farm near Pontypool, working her butt off all day, equally and alongside Dad, in a rapidly failing attempt to make enough money to survive on. Mam had eight siblings. Why had she drawn the short straw? Letters with the little blue telltale *par avion* stickers would often appear from aunties and uncles who'd left Holland after the war to find their fortunes in California, Canada, and other exotic outreaches, and Mam would devour them for weeks. Pontypool? And a pig farm? It wasn't the high life, and no doubt didn't quite fit Granddad's (Opa's) thinking either, who was highly concerned at the prospect after Dad had proposed. He wouldn't have thought much of a farmer's prospects unless it was some grand estate of rolling downs where it took a week to walk the boundaries. Persondy was a dilapidated 40-acre smallholding, most of which was either on a big slope, or ancient woodland.

It had all started as an idyllic picture-book farmstead. So maybe Opa might have thought it romantic and perhaps it fitted into some aspect of his Christian philosophical theory. In those early days it even had some grass around the place and at least the look of a 'farm'. But it didn't stand a chance of working, even when Mam arrived in 1955, and even though the post-war government had actively encouraged agricultural development.

It was about 1973 when things started to change, when

his patriarchal position was still unquestioned, but when the days of Dad working outdoors from dawn to dusk started closing in. The farm started changing from that point as well. In 1947 Dad had completed his HND at Rhadyr, Usk, in 'dairying', so he knew the practical basics of farming, but had no background in business. When the farm was at its lowest point – around 1964/5 – the bank forced them to sell most of the land. So they decided that Mam would farm Persondy on the limited ground that was left, and Dad went to work for Cecil Jenkins at Mamheilad House, a ten-minute walk across fields to the north. That didn't work out after Dad was caught pinching some of Jenkins' animal feed to help Mam's livestock at home. So Dad returned to farm the desperately inadequate operation that remained at Persondy.

Mam's flurry with the minibuses was the catalyst for change. She had been enticed into that by 'Uncle George' – one of the 'Vater' families of Abergavenny – who I suspect had a soft spot for Mam, but who I also suspect was deeply sympathetic for their plight. He needed more drivers for his minibus business and Mam was available and willing. And then, once Dad realised Mam was making more money driving kids to school a few hours a day than he was, working morning till night, he packed it all in and joined her. Uncle George wasn't concerned about the possible competition (Dad and Mam would have laughed at that idea!) and indeed did what he could to help them. He was an interesting character, with a 'Home Guard' background and a fierce devotion to Labour politics, so no doubt there was a bond there with Dad.

So Dad chucked in the towel as far as the farm was concerned, brought in his mate to bulldoze down the farm buildings and to 'landscape' the land around the house and barn, and settled into a life pootling round in his minibus each morning and evening, usually ferrying school kids.

What that did was give him time to spend on his other interests, and foremost among those were his gardening and carpentry.

Persondy became a listed building in 1975. By that stage Dad had already significantly restored it, bringing in old oak beams from a demolished house elsewhere, and then carving them to match the joists that had been removed by previous owners. He re-installed an enormous oak fireplace lintel which had been abandoned in a nearby field and recreated the original west window which had been replaced by a curious Georgian sash arrangement. The house was starting to become something of real merit. And the gardens changed altogether as well. There had been no 'garden' to speak of before – only swathes of earth which the pigs had 'mooted up' and acres of pigshit, as there was no room for a proper sewage system. But there were lots of farm buildings, however, so once they went the opportunity to create a large garden was evident and Dad was good at the Capability Brown thing. Indeed, his landscaping talent is now there for all to see – mature groups of trees and shrubbery, located where they best created a showpiece setting. He had no money for grand landscaped gestures of course, so he fine-tuned a great art in pinching cuttings from other places and 'borrowing' a tree or two. Persondy has a fine line of silver birch up its driveway, which look very similar to those planted by the Forestry Commission up in the wood above the house.

But even though the house and garden were starting to become something quite beautiful, that didn't stop the mishaps with his driving – like meeting me head-on at Croes y Pant corner one Sunday morning or, more alarmingly, veering wildy across the main A4042 in the face of oncoming traffic, to pick me up when I was waiting on the other side of the road after rugby training. I opened the minibus door horrified.

He sat back casually and smiled, 'maybe you'd better take over the driving now son'.

He got lost once, after driving a set of kids to school. Totally lost, not just going out of his way. He ended up miles away off course, and spent hours trying to work out where he was. In the end Mam drove out and miraculously found him, but it scared him and Mam, and he stopped the 'school run' soon after.

Because, although gardening and carpentry were now his real interests – and the improvements to the landscape (evidenced by more visitors, even the rest of the family – whatever next!) and the house were testament to that – the decline was starting and perhaps Dad knew it.

He started falling over. Not once or twice but on increasing occasions. 'Good job his rugby days taught him how to fall,' said Mam – though I suspect those were Dad's words of comfort, not hers. Sometimes I'd look out of the window and watch him fall, and with Persondy's land on a slope it didn't take much to start it off. Like something out of a Charlie Chaplin episode, I'd see him sliding past the window at an angle as he desperately sought to right himself, and hear the thud a few seconds later as his shoulder hit the ground. He'd get up laughing, apparently unhurt, but I had my doubts.

And as his physical demeanour changed, so did his mental one. It was slow of course, but soon we knew he couldn't carry on. Mam could, but she was 14 years younger and fit. His diet (nightly cheese on toast, after a gigantic supper), sedentary lifestyle and a total lack of interest in physical exercise ('did enough of that in the war') finally caught up with him. So for all the emerging beauty of Persondy's garden, Dad ended up glued to his chair in front of the fire with Harold Robbins, speaking to no-one, and with only the occasional limited greeting to Mam, Jant or me.

It got too much for Mam, not just physically but mentally too, and she organised for him to be taken into care at the County Hospital in Panteg. I remember helping her when she dropped him off – he was still in his total silence – and then seeing her weeping as she drove home with me. She couldn't stand it, and before long I was back there with her to collect him. He met us at the top of the stairs in his PJs (where did they come from? He never owned any.), complaining that everyone there was mad and when could he go home? Well, at least he was talking. He came home, and Mam made up a bed for him in Persondy's living room.

And there he stayed, in that same bed, for around five years – probably five more than he might have lived had he stayed at the County Hospital – and Mam took total care of him, feeding, washing, everything, interspersed with help from Jant and Helen, my wife. It didn't help his aversion to communication and that drove Mam mad, but she couldn't live without him, just as much as he couldn't without her.

They had created something of beauty out of nothing. In his will he gave everything to Mam, but in financial terms it was a pittance and she ended up eeking out an extremely frugal existence for another 20 years. But she'd had plenty of practice at that, and indeed didn't want anything different. In the end there were things which, to her, were more important.

Each other. Amsterdam and Wales, in a union for life.

CHAPTER 11

Hanny

In memoriam

Alan Francis

THE IDYLL IS finally over. On the morning of Sunday, 3 May 2020, Mam left us quietly, in Persondy, and with her she took the last remnants of Dad and closed the final chapter on an amazing life and a remarkable love affair.

Her timing was impeccable. It was 20 years, almost to the day, since Dad had died. I never really thought about it, but now she's gone I can see that he was still by her side continuously for those last 20 years, and she never wanted him to leave her.

It was why she cared for him so diligently during the last five years of his life when he was bedridden; why she took him back from local respite care so that he didn't have to be away from Persondy, and why she struggled to make new friends afterwards (she'd become too used to his reclusive ways).

When he went, most of her went too, and though she

occasionally broke away after his death, travelling to California, Canada and Holland, it was to Persondy she wanted to return, and where she felt closest to him.

She was often deeply unhappy during those last two decades and hard to please, as if the strain of separation was somehow unjust. Over the course of 45 years they had developed a little citadel together. Now that dream is over, and she has joined him where she would have wanted to be all along.

*

Like all the Dooyeweerd women, Mam was a beauty, a real looker, and also a perfectionist. She was a very capable musician and a talented artist. But like her mother, she was also a very practical woman. Occupied Amsterdam and her wartime life on the north Holland farms were, essentially, where all her practicalities were learnt and they never left her.

And so, although she had enjoyed a middle class, academic and even a noble upbringing, she was also a survivor – something Dad desperately needed on a small subsistence farm. When she was young she could play many of Rachmaninoff's piano concertos from memory, but in her married life her aesthetic sensibilities prevented her from bringing a piano into Persondy.

She would complain that they couldn't afford one, which was no doubt true; that Dad didn't want her playing and disturbing his fireside reading (possibly also true), but I suspect it was also her own concern that an upright piano (no room for a grand) wouldn't look right in the restored sixteenth-century interior.

She did find her musical outlet later in life when she acquired a small electric piano, but when I went to look for it recently I found it wrapped up and stored away. It still didn't look right in the living room, I guess. She was still worried, perhaps, that Dad would frown looking at it.

Even though they were joined at the hip, Mam was always fiercely independent and although she would often defer to his more senior knowledge, she was never under Dad's thumb. She was proud and very, very strong, and even though 14 years his junior, to a large extent she ran the household.

Not that such an idea was new – it was often how our local farms operated: the man outside doing the physical stuff and the woman taking care of finances and the house. But Mam and Dad were different, as she spent just as much time outside as him and, when the farm idea lost its way, it was Mam who took the initiative to break into new things. She had no time for pathos, and was always a 'doer' not a 'thinker'.

She didn't take kindly to pets – 'dogs need to stay outside' – and ran the house strictly. We all knew where we stood. It was a robust, rural household – not a shred of suburbanity – but with everything in its place, and everything done in immaculate taste, if not with any financial foundation.

She loved men. She had some great female friends who stayed with her to the end, but her praise was always reserved for the males. Where did that come from? For all his international fame as a philosophical theoretician, her father was a difficult man who only tolerated his children in small doses.

He was, nevertheless, delighted that Mam had passed her final exams at school – at that point the only one of her siblings to do so. He saw great things for her. No doubt, Persondy probably didn't quite fit his vision!

As a teenager she would seek counsel from him, waiting patiently outside his study until he replied to her gentle knock on the door. She had chosen Gandhi as a dissertation topic and naturally believed that her Christian philosopher father would help her with her work, but he hated the idea and told her so. She was told to leave but she protested.

She would likewise often back her mother up when her father took issue. Once she addressed him a little flippantly – 'Hi Dad!', tapping him on the shoulder. He pulled her up in no uncertain terms. She needed to show more respect. Did she crave his affection in the face of such paternal authority? Was that what triggered some lifelong male affection thing? It filtered through her life. I was the chosen one, and her grandson, son-in-law and grandson-in-law were the same. The girls always had it tougher.

Although Mam lived in Wales for 65 years, and from her accent you'd be forgiven for not realising that she was not born in the Gwent valleys, she held on to her Dutch passport all her life. One of her friends suggested recently that being Dutch helped her maintain independence, and it would certainly have helped create a strength in her during the early part of her time in Wales.

Her English was very poor when she arrived; she was a 19-year-old Continental beauty and the focus of many of the local lads' attentions (I always wondered why the Courts brothers were always at our place), but she always felt that she was an 'outsider' in the village.

She was the obvious culprit when Mrs Davies, our local shopkeeper, found a foreign coin in the till (never mind that it wasn't a Dutch one). Her English of course did improve (though tinged with Welsh dialect), but her mother tongue never left her at all, even when she went months without using Dutch at all, though five minutes after using it she would turn to my sister and I and continue in Dutch – something she and I never learnt to our shame. I think, largely, as Dad didn't approve of it around the house (British Army thinking?). When our children became fully bilingual later (Welsh/English), I could see a conflict within her – perhaps Dad was on her shoulder then as well, and perhaps it was a challenge to her – why hadn't she persevered with Dutch for us? We learnt the odd phrase of course – *mag ik de theelepel alsjeblieft* (can I have a teaspoon, please), *jij bent gek* (are you crazy) and indeed, especially towards the end, it tended to be 'Oma' rather than 'Mam'. It was perhaps fitting that the last thing she did, before retiring for the night when she died, was to watch a Dutch-language programme on TV with us. It was a complex drama (English sub-titles), and I wondered whether the modern Dutch would be too fast for her to follow, especially at midnight with a few whiskies under belt. She would have none of that! 'Of course I understood it all, Al. It's my language!'

Her partnership with Dad was blessed, so it's no surprise that life changed for her when he died. She was able to travel (Newport was a day out for him) and meet some new friends. Difficult at first of course, as her 'solitude' with Dad (the least sociable person in the world) didn't improve her social networking skills (how she hated that word!). But, in Colin, she found a great partner who she shared many years with, even though she would return home from a weekend together worried that she had overdone it on the alcohol front (not something that usually concerned her. She had a remarkably strong constitution, especially where whisky was concerned.).

Mam really did have a remarkable life. One of huge contrasts. A city lady from a well-to-do Amsterdam family who revelled in life on a small subsistence farm in the back of beyond. She brought her own special creativity to the partnership – Persondy became forever tinged with Dutchness – fields of orange. She was intensely controlling in many ways, yet Jant and I enjoyed a very loving childhood with almost no restrictions on where we spent our time. Mam could be up to her eyes in cow/chicken/pig muck for large parts of the day and yet emerge for the evening beautifully made up, and with an immaculately presented spread of food ready on the table (milk in a proper milk jug please Al, not the carton). She could play Chopin from memory, but spent large parts of her time in outdoor working clothes.

But, of everything, my lasting memory was that Jant and I had the luck to be born into a family home which was full of love. We didn't have a lot, and during the early years, especially, Mam and Dad were outside for most of the time and not with us. But there was always affection in large amounts, and we'll miss it enormously. Mam was at the centre of that.

Postscript

Jantien Powell (née Francis) is a professional artist and tutor. After several years spent teaching, she set up Chapel Cottage Studio in 2008 at her home in Llanddewi Rhydderch, near Abergavenny, which she shares with husband David, and, in a separate annexe, her daughter Tirza, husband Richard Snook and their children, Caian and Nia. Jantien's other daughter, Jessica, lives independently in Abergavenny.

*

Alan Francis is an architect and co-founder of Gaunt Francis Architects in Cardiff. Together with his wife Helen they now live in Persondy's adjacent barn (Ysguborwen) which they converted in the early 1990s. They have two children, Iestyn and Rhiannon, who live in Bristol and Cardiff respectively.

*

Stephen Jones was born in Newport, Gwent, and is a journalist and rugby correspondent with *The Sunday Times*. He has won the UK Sports Journalist of the Year award, has twice been UK Sports Correspondent of the Year and three times Rugby Writer of the Year. He has also covered golf, racing, football and cricket for *The Sunday Times*. This is his first foray into non-sporting literature.

*

Persondy is a Grade II* listed building, one of only two in Mamheilad, which together with Grade I buildings make up only four per cent of the listed buildings in Wales (the remaining 96 per cent being Grade II). Its importance can be measured by its inclusion in several books about historic buildings, including Fox & Raglan's *Monmouthshire Houses*, Peter Smith's *Houses of the Welsh Countryside*, Pevsner's *Buildings of Wales* and Hando's *Out and About in Monmouthshire*. The adjacent barn, Ysguborwen, is listed Grade II.

*

Mamheilad is a small hamlet on the outskirts of Pontypool. The derivation of this old Welsh name has been lost over time, and it is now more usually spelt without its 'e' – Mamhilad – but most historical books and many old maps include the 'e', so it is included here for authenticity. Alan is currently campaigning for the lost 'e' to be re-introduced. It makes pronouniation easier for visitors – the middle syllable, which is the emphasis, should sound like 'high' not 'hill'.

*

Holland – throughout this book Hanny refers to 'Holland' when she means 'The Netherlands'. To her they were both the same. Maybe that was because she was an Amsterdam girl, and therefore within the province called 'Holland' on the western coast of the Netherlands. Alan pressed her on it once, but she didn't give in. Holland it is then.